LEARNING TRACKS

SAGE was founded in 1965 by Sara Miller McCune to support the dissemination of usable knowledge by publishing innovative and high-quality research and teaching content. Today, we publish over 900 journals, including those of more than 400 learned societies, more than 800 new books per year, and a growing range of library products including archives, data, case studies, reports, and video. SAGE remains majority-owned by our founder, and after Sara's lifetime will become owned by a charitable trust that secures our continued independence.

Los Angeles | London | New Delhi | Singapore | Washington DC

LEARNING TRACKS

planning and assessing learning for children with severe and complex needs

LINDY FURBY & JILLY CATLOW

Los Angeles | London | New Delhi
Singapore | Washington DC

Los Angeles | London | New Delhi
Singapore | Washington DC

SAGE Publications Ltd
1 Oliver's Yard
55 City Road
London EC1Y 1SP

SAGE Publications Inc.
2455 Teller Road
Thousand Oaks, California 91320

SAGE Publications India Pvt Ltd
B 1/I 1 Mohan Cooperative Industrial Area
Mathura Road
New Delhi 110 044

SAGE Publications Asia-Pacific Pte Ltd
3 Church Street
#10-04 Samsung Hub
Singapore 049483

Editor: Amy Jarrold
Assistant editor: George Knowles
Production editor: Tom Bedford
Marketing manager: Dilhara Attygalle
Cover design: Wendy Scott
Typeset by: C&M Digitals (P) Ltd, Chennai, India
Printed and bound by CPI Group (UK) Ltd,
    Croydon, CR0 4YY

Library of Congress Control Number: 2015943061

British Library Cataloguing in Publication data

A catalogue record for this book is available from the British Library

ISBN 978-1-4739-1252-6
ISBN 978-1-4739-1253-3 (pbk)

At SAGE we take sustainability seriously. Most of our products are printed in the UK using FSC papers and boards. When we print overseas we ensure sustainable papers are used as measured by the PREPS grading system. We undertake an annual audit to monitor our sustainability.

Contents

About the Authors

Lindy Furby has had a long and interesting career in education. She taught at two primary schools in Brixton, London. She then became a primary maths consultant for the Inner London Education Authority; her job was to encourage enthusiastic mathematics teaching. To facilitate her work, she took an Open University degree in Mathematics (and cried her way through summer school – she is not a natural mathematician). Next, she moved to Bradford to become a senior lecturer in maths and mathematics education and gained a Masters degree in Maths and Maths Education. After twelve years, another move to the North took her to Edinburgh, where she briefly taught at an infant school and then started work at St Crispin's special school. She found the work enjoyable but very challenging, and took many courses including a Diploma in Autism and Forest School Leadership in her effort to improve the outcomes of her teaching. Now she has retired and spends her time skiing, mountaineering, ski touring, painting, printmaking, travelling and, recently, writing a book.

Jilly Catlow has been teaching in special education for eight years. As a trained primary teacher, she always knew that she wanted to work in special education, originally with children with social, emotional and behavioural difficulties, and autism. Learning disability was something that Jilly was initially introduced to in her first mainstream class with a little girl with moderate learning disabilities. This interest grew quickly and Jilly began working at St Crispin's two years later. As a relatively inexperienced teacher, especially for severe and complex learning disabilities, Jilly was lucky enough to have Lindy in the classroom next door. They formed a fast friendship and a fantastic working relationship which they supported and challenged each other to learn and develop. To extend her understanding, Jilly undertook a Post-graduate Certificate in Child and Young People's Mental Health and Psychological Practice, with qualifications in child development, learning disability and challenging behaviour. Over the time at St Crispin's, Jilly has specialised in communication and positive behavioural support, and is now one of the school's principal teachers.

Acknowledgements

We would like to thank the children and young people, their parents and all the staff at St Crispin's, Edinburgh, including speech and language therapists and the occupational therapist. Without their help this book would not exist.

Additional Resources

With your purchase of this book you have been given access to the readymade assessment booklet **Learning Tracks**. This is available as a PDF with editable elements and a blank template Word document so you can personalise it to suit your individual needs.

You can access your customisable Learning Tracks booklet in a few simple steps.

Step 1: Visit https://study.sagepub/learningtracks

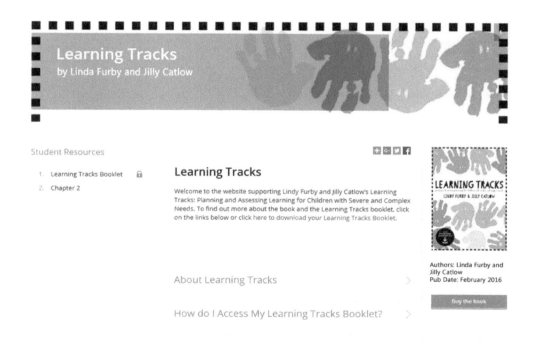

Step 2: Create or log into your SAGE account.

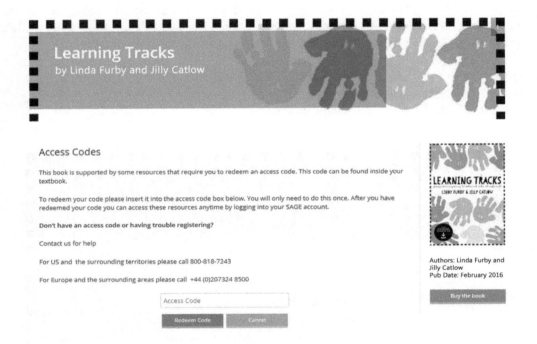

Step 3: Redeem your code. This can be found at the front of your book.

Step 4: Start using your booklet.

Introduction

Learning Tracks is an online, printable planning and tracking booklet written to support the planning and assessment of learning for children and young people with **severe and complex learning disabilities (SCLD)**. It was designed by Lindy Furby and Jilly Catlow while teaching at St Crispin's School for children and young people with severe and complex learning disabilities in Edinburgh. This book is a companion to the booklet.

At the very early stages of learning, the steps that children and young people make can be small but incredibly significant for them and those who teach them. However, it can be problematic to evidence and formally recognise these achievements and plan next steps. *Learning Tracks* presents a framework to recognise achievement at these early levels and plan for progression through challenge, breadth and application.

The *Learning Tracks* framework for recognising achievement at very early levels of learning:

- can help teachers understand the way their children may be learning;
- offers a vocabulary for describing the learning;
- offers a structure for planning the learning.

This framework is based on an extended Bloom's *Taxonomy* (Bloom et al., 1956).

Learning Tracks was written specifically for our school in Edinburgh. We shared the booklet at the Scottish Festival in 2013 and it was suggested there that it might be helpful to share it with a wider audience – hence the book.

In Part 1, we explain the theories underpinning *Learning Tracks*; in Part 2, we describe the curriculum included in *Learning Tracks*; and in Part 3, we demonstrate how *Learning Tracks* can be used for recording and planning the learning of children and young people with severe and complex learning disabilities. Throughout the book, references to particular sections of *Learning Tracks* in the online material are made using codes – for example, H3 (Health and Wellbeing 3); these sections can be accessed online using the search feature and the code. After this Introduction, we introduce six case study children who are used as examples in the rest of the book.

What are severe and complex learning disabilities (SCLDs)?

In the United Kingdom, children with learning disabilities are categorised into four groups: mild, moderate, severe and profound. One way of describing these four groups is by **Intelligence Quotient (IQ)** scores where an IQ score of:

- 50–70 = mild learning disabilities;
- 35–50 = moderate learning disabilities;
- 20–35 = severe learning disabilities;
- less than 20 = profound learning disabilities.

However, in practice, children are usually assessed by professional observation of behaviour, not by IQ testing.

Complex learning disabilities are **comorbid** with conditions such as an **autistic spectrum disorder (ASD)**, **Down's syndrome**, **fragile X syndrome (FXS)**, **attention deficit hyperactivity disorder (ADHD)**, **tuberous sclerosis**, epilepsy and **attachment disorder**.

St Crispin's is a state special school for children aged 5–18 with severe and complex learning disabilities. Some 50 of the 54 children also have a diagnosis of an autistic spectrum disorder. There are nine classes with a maximum of six children with a class team of one teacher, one nursery nurse and two pupil support assistants, and an occasional class has extra staffing when required. There are three part-time specialist teachers, for PE, art and music, four days a week of speech therapy, one day of occupational therapy and physiotherapy when required, a head teacher and a depute head teacher.

No initial teacher training for special needs is offered in Scotland. The teachers in the school are qualified as primary or secondary teachers, and when they start working at the school most are lacking both in experience (due to the low incidence of the children) and qualifications in special needs.

The children and young people present with a wide range of abilities and disabilities. Nearly all our pupils are physically able; they can walk, run and climb; they can sit on chairs when they feel like it; their eyesight and hearing are generally excellent (especially for crisp packets). All our pupils have serious problems with communication. Many have no spoken language; some have a little spoken language; all have difficulties understanding spoken language in a range from understanding no spoken language, to understanding simple familiar sentences in familiar contexts. As a result of their communication disabilities, most of our pupils present with challenging behaviour. Most of our pupils have **sensory processing difficulties (or sensory integration difficulties)**. In terms of life skills, a few come to school with toileting skills, but most don't; a few can undress themselves but the majority of pupils, throughout the school, need help with dressing. Around 50 per cent of the children have been referred to the **Child and Adolescent Mental Health Service (CAMHS)** generally in the senior school as their behaviour becomes less manageable due to their size.

Children and young people with SCLD are very rare. The incidence rate is 0.001 per cent of the population for children with severe learning disabilities. In Edinburgh, this implies that of the 75,000 children between 0 and 15 years of age, there will be 75 children with severe learning disabilities before one even starts to add the concept of complexities. This makes it difficult in developing and sharing good practices for helping them to learn; there simply aren't that many people working with them.

History of education of children with severe and complex learning disabilities

Although Scotland and England have different educational philosophies and systems, there are some similarities in their history of education.

Under the 1944 Education Act (England) and 1945 Education Act (Scotland), children with special educational needs were categorised by their disabilities defined in medical terms. Children with severe and complex learning disabilities were considered 'uneducable and untrainable' and were 'cared for' in day centres and hospitals.

The 1970 Education Act (England) and 1974 Education Act (Scotland) removed the use of the terms 'ineducable' and 'untrainable'. All children became entitled to an education provided by an education authority. So children and young people with severe and complex learning disabilities have been going to school in the United Kingdom for 40 years.

In the 1990s, both England and Scotland introduced national curricula for all pupils. In Scotland, this curriculum was further developed for the needs of special education by the elaborated curriculum. In England, P levels were introduced in 2011 for planning and assessing the learning of children working below Level 1 of the national curriculum.

Both countries have a new national curriculum: *A Curriculum for Excellence* was published in Scotland in 2004; and in England, the new National Curriculum was published in 2014. In England, the P levels documentation was also revised for 'pupils aged 5–16 with special educational needs (SEN) who cannot access the National Curriculum' (DES, 2014: 3), however, in Scotland it was stated that there was no intention to have an elaborated curriculum for the Curriculum for Excellence.

As a result of the low incidence of children with SEN, most teachers who start working in our school have had no experience of these children. These children have only been educated in Scotland and England for the last 40 years, and although this seems a long time, it is not long enough to build up a wealth of available knowledge of different ways of engaging these children in learning. In our experience, new teachers starting work in our school need support with:

- finding out what the children can know/can do;
- deciding on what the children/young people should learn;
- planning for learning;
- teaching to the plans.

These are the reasons why we designed *Learning Tracks*.

Bold words are included in the Glossary. Only the first instance of each glossary term in the book is in bold.

References

Bloom, B., Englehart, M.D., Furst, E.J., Hill, W.H. and Krathwohl, D. (1956) *Taxonomy of Educational Objectives Handbook 1.* New York: Longmans.

DES (July 2014) *Performance – P Scale – Attainment Targets for Children with Special Educational Needs* (www.gov.uk/government/publications/p-scales-attainment-targets-for-pupils-with-sen, accessed 25 August 2014).

Case Studies

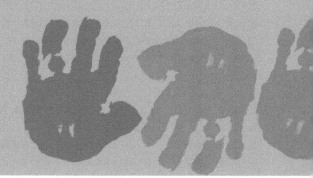

Case studies can offer a picture of the children we work with. We have chosen six young people in the senior school because we have a timeline of knowledge of these young people. Most of the likes, dislikes, obsessions, triggers and behaviours are shared by many of the pupils of all ages in the school and anybody working with children with severe and complex learning disabilities will recognise their profiles in an instant. We will use these children and young people to present examples throughout the book. Their names have obviously been changed.

1 Andrew

Name	Andrew	
Age	17	
Diagnosis	ASD, **Severe Learning Disability (SLD)** an **Adaptive Behaviour Assessment System (ABAS)** cognitive age of 18 months. He has been referred to CAMHS.	
Likes/obsessions	Playing with lentils, small beads, etc., Thomas the Tank Engine – which is such a common like/obsession with children with an ASD, that it is jokingly considered an autistic diagnosis instrument in itself (National Autistic Society) – silky materials, catalogues (particularly food catalogues, especially at Christmas), being outside, crisps (favourite thing in the world – a great motivator), smelling people, travelling on the school bus, and lounging around on floor cushions like a Roman emperor.	
Dislikes/triggers	Noise – Andrew wears **ear defenders** which are special earphones designed to cut out noise – busy places, change, being messy, having his hair, finger and toenails cut, changes in routines, things not being expected, pain, illness, constipation, and waiting.	
Communication	Speech receptive (i.e. what spoken words he understands)	Very limited understanding of speech, what he does understand is heavily supported by context and gesture.
	Speech expressive (i.e. what he can say)	No speech.
	Signing	Limited to the sign for 'please' for *everything* – e.g. give it to me or take it away.
	Symbols receptive	About 20 known symbols. He can learn other symbols but needs constant revision and use to maintain them; he forgets them very easily.
	Symbols expressive	He uses about 10 symbols consistently. He understands the **Picture Exchange Communication System (PECS)** process (where a small symbol is exchanged for a desired object). He will also travel across a room to an adult with his symbol in order to acquire a desired object.
School learning	Andrew does not read or write and cannot count. He is, however, very good at matching and sorting.	

(Continued)

(Continued)

Name	Andrew	
Self-care	Toileting	Andrew was toilet-trained at 12 years of age but still has accidents mainly due to communication difficulties – i.e. he cannot always tell us he needs to go.
	Dressing	Can do everything except fiddly buttons and zips.
	Eating	Andrew can be obsessional about food – he is a raider – and searches cupboards mainly for crisps and biscuits but has been known to eat raw sausage. He will take food from other people's plates, which causes lots of issues in shops, school, home and the community. Otherwise he eats well and widely.
	Travel	No awareness of danger or of anything standing between him and his desires. If he wants something, he just pushes everything and everyone out of the way. He loves travelling on buses but needs 2:1 ratio of staffing when travelling on public buses.
Behaviour		When distressed, he grabs people on the underside of their upper arm. If that has no result, he escalates to ripping upper clothing off the adults helping him and lastly he bites hard. Unusually for our school he sometimes targets other children, usually in an attempt to quieten their noise.
Calming strategies		Relaxation routine consisting of four songs, hand massage and then just lying down relaxing next to his carer. Deep pressure massage, designed by our occupational therapist (OT), especially squeezes to his shoulders.
Rewards		Lentils and crisps for really big things like being seen by the doctor, having his hair or nails cut.

Anecdote

A description of a typical happy interaction: Andrew is lounging on floor cushions in the sensory room next to the mirror so that he can watch himself play with lentils. This play consists of taking a fistful of lentils out of a box, holding them high above his head and sprinkling them back into the box, which is his favourite activity. He sees a trusted member of staff, gets up, crosses the room, pulls her across the room to sit with him and gives her an affectionate sniff.

2 Ewan

Name	Ewan	
Age	17	
Diagnosis	ASD, SLD and an ABAS cognitive age of 2 years. He has been referred to CAMHS.	
Likes/obsessions	Trains, feathers, slinkies, fluttering little bits of thread, walking; he really likes being outside, crisps, chocolate buttons, trusted people – he comes up and taps people he trusts. He likes people to say familiar phrases.	
Dislikes/triggers	Change, passing a bowel movement, being changed after problems with passing a bowel movement (many children and young people with autism have significant bowel problems which causes a lot of pain and distress – 50% of the school are on medication for such problems), sitting especially when constipated, drinking (his medicine used to be put in his drinks – and he saw it), wearing shoes, new places, new people, not enough structure, thinking about a negative incident, and waiting.	
Communication	Speech receptive	Understands speech in context, he can follow up to 2 familiar **Information Carrying Words (ICW**; Knowles and Masidlover, 1982) – e.g. 'Give me the red bus', where the choice is a red bus, a green bus, a red car and a green car – the information carrying words are 'red/green' and 'bus/car'.
	Speech expressive	Can use about 20 words, but his pronunciation is only understood by people who know him well.
	Signing	Has about 5–10 signs he uses, but some are completely idiosyncratic – e.g. he taps his throat when something hurts and the something is usually his head.
	Symbols receptive	Has a good understanding of symbols, probably 100 receptive. He learns symbols very quickly and retains them.
	Symbols expressive	Uses about 50 symbols regularly and spontaneously. He can do 3-part requests. He is an expert user of his symbolic timetable throughout the day which has transformed his understanding of what is going on. He also uses sub-**schedules** to break down activities, especially outings; now that he is aware of what is going to happen, he can go to new places.
School learning	Cannot read or write words, but he can make and read sentences with symbols. He can recognise his own name. He can rote count to 20 and give numbers of objects to 10. He is also good at matching and sorting.	

(Continued)

(Continued)

Name	Ewan	
Self-care	Toileting	Toilet-trained but has massive problems with constipation; he used only to empty his bowels in the bath (not uncommon with children with these problems).
	Dressing	Can dress and undress himself and has gradually over the years learnt to accept shoes; for many years he would break the backs down and shuffle around in the resulting clog-like shoe. He now wears shoes properly.
	Eating	Has difficulty eating with others. He only eats dry food, and different foods on the plate must not touch each other. He used to refuse all drinks and obtained all his fluid from oranges. He had seen someone add his medication to a drink. He is very suspicious of food and drink.
	Travel	Loves the bus. He has learnt road-safety rules; he will walk nicely with an adult, will stop at the corner, knows the red man stop, green man go, but we are not sure about his level of understanding of danger. He likes to know where he is going and to be accompanied by a trusted adult.
Behaviour		Has shown a massive improvement in the last 4 years.
		Up to 12 years of age: he displayed distress through punching, kicking and head-butting really hard, and running away. He could not tolerate direction, working with others in a group or individual work. The only place he was happy was outside, as far away from everybody else as possible, twiddling his threads in the breeze. He was scared and suspicious of everything and everyone.
		Now: he still displays these behaviours when he is in discomfort or things aren't right for him but he has better ways of getting his needs met and has learnt to trust people and enjoy being with them. He still uses a **comforter** to help him deal with difficult situations; his present favoured comforter is a slinky.
Calming strategies		Bouncing on a physio ball, reassuring touch, having his hand held or his head rubbed.
Rewards		Choosing time after each activity, feathers, slinky, string, floaty materials and being outside.

Anecdote 1

A recent big achievement: Ewan used his symbol timetable to catch two consecutive buses to go bowling (a new activity), to have lunch there and catch two buses back to school without recourse to his slinky because he was happy and relaxed.

Anecdote 2

The best anecdote is just to see Ewan run up to a trusted adult who had left the school and was visiting, with a big smile on his face, happy to see her.

3 Isla

Name	Isla	
Age	13	
Diagnosis	Down's syndrome, ASD and SCLD.	
Likes/obsessions	Attention on any terms. If she cannot get it by positive behaviour she will get it by negative behaviour. She loves tickles, water play, messy play – the messier the better – **Forest School**, outings and trips, *Fabby Dabby Dee* (a song), singing, cake and throwing things.	
Dislikes/triggers	Unpredictability, lack of attention, being cleaned particularly after toileting, babies (she scratches babies to make them predictable), and waiting.	
Communication	Speech receptive	Can understand familiar speech in familiar contexts supported by symbols.
	Speech expressive	.Uses about 20 nouns, but they are very difficult to understand due to her pronunciation.
	Signing	Can use around 15 signs, although they are small and very idiosyncratic. Spontaneously she uses only the signs for cake and bread (and all the signs to *Fabby Dabby Dee*).
	Symbols receptive	Has a very good understanding of symbols; she recognises over 100 and learns new symbols easily.
	Symbols expressive	Is a good PECS user at a three-words level. She has a vocabulary of over 50 words. Sadly, the urge to throw things gets in the way of communication at times.

(Continued)

Name	Isla	
School learning	Can say the numbers to 10 by rote but she cannot count objects. She is good at 1:1 correspondence and sorting. She can recognise her own name (written).	
Self-care	Toileting	Generally has control but she is a behavioural wetter. She has naturally loose bowels and when she is anxious, she loses control of her bowels and then she hates getting cleaned.
	Dressing	Independent with simple clothing.
	Eating	Is obsessional about food. She will eat anything. She mouths everything and explores the world with her tongue. Her favourite food is cake – she loves cake.
	Travel	Loves travelling and being outside. However, she has no sense of danger, is very fast on her feet and all her joints are hyper-flexible. She needs a staffing ratio of 2:1 on outings.
Behaviour	Behavioural wetting for attention-seeking and escape from any scary new task or boring task, if not engaged or having to wait. She scratches eyes and glasses seeking reactions, attention and predictability. She strips off her clothes really fast and is so flexible that she can wriggle her way out of any all-in-one garment designed to keep her clothed.	
Calming strategies/ rewards	An adult singing to her, 1:1 attention in a quiet space, praise. She loves praise.	

Anecdote

Isla loves structured relaxation. She will sit on the floor in a group listening to music enjoying a hand massage. She will look her adult straight in the eye, take the back of their hand and kiss it (or lick it – same meaning) and nestle in for a cuddle.

4 Donald

Name	Donald	
Age	16	
Diagnosis	ASD, SCLD, attachment disorder and **dyspraxia** affecting fine and gross motor control and speech. He has been referred to CAMHS.	
Likes/obsessions	Snoozes (an imaginative play routine where he rests his head on a carer's shoulders, shuts his eyes and snores, and the carer rests his/her head on his head and snores too, which calms him down and also makes a great reward), hiccups, being outside, Argos catalogues, iPad, particular DVDs, and the *X Factor*.	
Dislikes/triggers	Leaving home, change, noise (he wears ear defenders), unpredictability of other people, he can be tactile defensive and textures can distress him (not always), the dark, previous bad experiences (tends to repeat bad experiences) and being told off.	
Communication	Speech receptive	Understands familiar speech in familiar contexts. Can follow familiar 2–3 ICW instructions.
	Speech expressive	Has around 100 words, but his speech is very unclear (dyspraxic), which causes a lot of frustration. He is not really helped by either symbols or **Voice Output Communication Aids (tablet, iPads) (VOCA)** because of the dyspraxia.
	Signing	Uses 'finished'.
	Symbols receptive	Recognises over 100 symbols.
	Symbols expressive	Dyspraxia causes problems for using symbols.
School learning	Reading: he used to read a reading scheme but now uses school-made books as the reading scheme quickly became too complex. He can build CVC (consonant-vowel-consonant) words. He recognises his own name. He can make sentences using symbols and words. He cannot write. He can count to 50 and understands numbers to 20. He is good at matching and sorting.	
Self-care	Toileting	In pads. He is aware of being wet or soiled and can ask to be changed but has no other awareness.
	Dressing	Dyspraxic, can pull things on with support. Unfortunately, refuses to wear joggers; he only likes proper trousers.
	Eating	Used to eat only sausages. Now eats anything except dairy (dislikes dairy). Sausages, chips and beans make him *really* happy.
	Travel	Likes the school bus. Uses the public bus with carers but finds it a major anxiety at school. Road safety: knows the red and green man but has no sense of safety. Needs to know *exactly* where he is going and who is accompanying him; he needs to trust that person wholly.

(Continued)

Name	Donald
Behaviour	Massive improvement in the last 3 years. Up to 13 years he displayed distress by scratching, extreme hair-pulling, biting, kicking and wrecking his environment. The first thing to go were his glasses, which is a signifier to people working with him. These behaviours reappear occasionally at times of extreme stress. He has spent 6 months being educated in an open shelter in the playground because he was too anxious to enter the school building.
Calming strategies	Snoozes, ear defenders, structured choice (he always has a choice of activity to give him an opt-out clause, so the activity will happen but he can do it outside if he wants).
Rewards	Outside, praise, snoozes, attention, use of familiar positive phrases – e.g. 'good day at school'.

Anecdote

He went to the theatre for the pantomime last year and although he had a **social story** of what was going to happen, he could not see an escape route and he had a massive meltdown. This year he pre-visited the theatre before the pantomime and he was given choices all the way through.

Choice 1: school or theatre – he chose theatre.

Choice 2: theatre or bus – he chose theatre.

Choice 3: upstairs or downstairs – he chose upstairs.

Choice 4: in auditorium or stairs – he chose stairs.

He enjoyed the performance from the stairs, peeping through the open door and listening to everything. All the way through it was emphasised that he could go back to the bus if he wanted. When he got back to school, he was completely elated and repeated and repeated, 'Good theatre, good theatre, good theatre.'

5 Dougal

Name	Dougal	
Age	16	
Diagnosis	ASD, SCLD, a notional cognitive age of 2½–3.	
Likes/obsessions	Trains, computers, being tickled, music, flapping poly pockets and making patterns in shaving foam and **cornflour gloop**.	
Dislikes/triggers	Noise, he is very sensitive to noise (he won't wear ear defenders), bowel movements, being cleaned after bowel movements, being messy or sticky, having the slightest mark on his clothes or the seams not being flat, change, unpredictability, waiting.	
Communication	Speech receptive	Understands familiar speech in familiar contexts. Can follow familiar 2–3 ICW instructions.
	Speech expressive	Dougal does not speak, but this has more to do with physical problems and actual delivery than his cognitive ability; he is verbally dyspraxic. He makes a lot of very expressive noises.
	Signing receptive	Understands signing and understands around 50 signs.
	Signing expressive	Due to his physical problems in speaking, Dougal is one of our few consistent signers and signing is used at home; he uses 20–30 signs independently – i.e. without prompting.
	Symbols receptive	Has a good understanding of symbolic communication; he can read sentences, follow instructions, and learns and remembers new symbols easily.
	Symbols expressive	Can answer questions with full symbol sentences; he can use symbols to make requests with distance, he can make comments. He is an accomplished communicator with symbols. He has an extensive vocabulary. Uses a VOCA – an aid that speaks when he presses programmed buttons or types in words – and can type familiar words (TV programmes, etc., that he doesn't have a symbol for).

(Continued)

(Continued)

Name	Dougal	
School learning	Has a very good understanding of numbers, including place value. Counting large numbers is difficult for him as he cannot speak but he understands large numbers and can use his VOCA for this. He can add and subtract up to 100. He has an understanding of the different values of coins. He can match times and has some understanding of time passing but is inconsistent in telling analogue time.	
	He can read and write at an Early level. He can read simple texts and has some knowledge of phonics. He can write his name independently and write simple familiar words – here he is restricted by poor fine motor control and can type familiar bigger words.	
Self-care	Toileting	Has been toilet-trained for a long time, but he has considerable problems with his bowels, both constipation and frequency; he wears a liner in his pants and is on medication. He usually deals with all his cleaning himself. All this causes him great distress.
	Dressing	Independent.
	Eating	Obsessive but no real issues with texture, etc.
	Travel	Travels well. He knows the rules for crossing roads and he has some sense of danger. The main problem for Dougal is noise: if there are loud noises or crying babies, this can cause him to become upset.
Behaviour	When distressed, he grabs people's arms or their hair. When very distressed, he will grab an adult's hair and pull them very close. He will head-butt or squeeze his forehead into the adult's face while screaming and stay like that. It is very hard to remove oneself from this position.	
Calming strategies/rewards	Watching trains on YouTube, poly pockets, a cape and deep-pressure head massage.	

Anecdote

When learning to use the Picture Exchange Communication System (PECS), we were having a party for someone's birthday and spontaneously Dougal presented us with 'I want green.' Knowing that one of Dougal's favourites was crisps, we gave him some of the salt-and-vinegar crisps (from a green packet). We were very excited by this, but when presented with the crisps Dougal didn't seem very excited but ate them. He repeated his presentation of 'I want green' and took the crisps but wasn't very pleased. He eventually presented us with 'I want green cake.' We looked at the table and saw that the caterpillar cake had a green-icing face. We were very excited and gave Dougal lots of praise and, of course, the cake. This was his first three-part sentence and was completely spontaneous. Sometimes we don't know the children as well as we think we do, and a bit of frustration brings on the communication.

6 Blair

Name	Blair	
Age	15	
Diagnosis	ASD, SCLD; his ABAS cognitive age is 3–4.	
Health	Has epilepsy (**tonic–clonic**) and **absences** currently (January 2015), one tonic–clonic seizure a month.	
Likes/obsessions	Washing machines, lifts, chat, greeting people (anybody), swimming, music, train game (a train-simulator game on the computer that does real-time real journeys), the TV programmes *Who Wants to be a Millionaire?*, *Countdown* and *Weakest Link*.	
Dislikes/triggers	Change, unpredictability, noise (occasionally wears ear defenders), things being broken, access to obsessions – i.e. lifts and washing machines, waiting, previous bad experiences (tends to repeat them), being told off.	
Communication	Speech receptive	When calm, he can follow up to 3 ICWs. He still needs a lot of support with symbols when he is stressed. He can understand most of what is said to him in familiar speech in a familiar context.
	Speech expressive	Lots of learnt language. All his speech has been learnt in phrases, although he uses these phrases appropriately. Blair uses **echolalic** speech (parroting of learnt phrases), although again he uses these phrases appropriately.
	Signing	Has about 10 signs he likes to use, particularly 'waiting' which he uses in an exaggerated theatrical way.

(Continued)

(Continued)

Name	Blair	
	Symbols receptive	Despite his understanding of speech, he still needs support from symbols, particularly when distressed. He has a very large vocabulary. While he understands a lot of language, he can't retain the instructions long enough to do the task – thus the need for symbols.
	Symbols expressive	Has been a very skilled PECS user but now speaks faster than he can make symbol sentences, which is the way he learnt to speak. He always uses symbol timetables; he needs everything broken down to the smallest degree, a full-day timetable and then numerous sub-schedules for every activity.
School learning	Literature: Blair understands that text has meaning. Initially, he learnt whole familiar words that were meaningful to him. After years of disinterested working on phonics, he suddenly started to use phonics to decode words last year. He can use lists of words but, due to anxiety, will not use them instead of symbol timetables and schedules yet. He can write his name but finds writing very difficult, both the planning of what to write and motor planning.	
	Maths: Blair has a good understanding of numbers. He can count to 1,000, knows his 2 and 10 times tables, can add 1 to any number and add any number to any number up to 20 on the number line.	
Self-care	Totally independent in toileting, dressing and food.	
	Travel	Knows the rules: says 'stop', looks each way (quite often towards the sky) and says, 'No cars, no cars, cross the road'; even if there are cars, he doesn't understand danger.
Behaviour	Runs for obsessions. He struggles to finish/leave things he likes doing, if somebody attempts to block the activity, he bites. He bangs the environment and his own head. He knows that banging windows gets a really good reaction. When upset, he can make himself vomit.	
Calming strategies	Structured relaxation, time in a quiet dark place, being wrapped up in a blanket, eating carbohydrates (crackers), 1:1 interaction and reassurance.	
Rewards	After each work activity choosing time; three times a day a special box with special music. End of the day a trip on the school lift.	

Anecdote

Blair has learnt that if he runs to grab things, he cannot have them. However, if he asks for things he can practically have them *all* the time.

So Blair was waiting for his class's turn at the bowling alley (Blair finds waiting hard) and he turned to Jilly and said, 'Jilly, I want to chase the pigeons.' Jilly said he couldn't, so he said much louder, 'I want to chase the pigeons!' Fortunately, it was his class's time for the bowling alley as this was something he couldn't really have, but he really thought he could have it as he had asked so nicely for it.

References

Knowles, W. and Masidlover, M. (1982) The Derbyshire Language Scheme. Published by Derbyshire County Council.
National Autistic Society (2001) *Children with Autism and Thomas the Tank Engine* (www.autism.org.uk/about-autism/our-publications/reports/our-policy-and-research-reports/children-with-autism-and-thomas-the-tank-engine.aspx, accessed 21 May 2015).

PART 1

The Theoretical Foundations of *Learning Tracks*

All teaching is based on theories of learning. These theories of learning might be intrinsic – that is, in the teacher's mind – not necessarily articulated or thought through, or extrinsic – that is, clearly considered and thought out. In this part, we discuss the theories underpinning *Learning Tracks*.

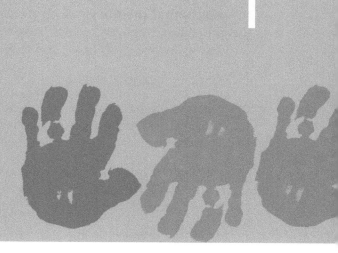

Learning and Memory

Learning is commonly defined as acquisition of knowledge and skills. Learning is an active process that starts with sensory input to the brain which is processed and stored in the memory. Further learning is achieved by modifying information already stored in the memory. At a cellular level in the brain, it is the formation of robust connections.

What is memory?

Memory is the ability to recall past experience and knowledge. As a result of increasingly sophisticated brain-scanning techniques, researchers are gradually discovering more and more about how the brain works, including how it remembers things. Much of this learning has come from studying people with brain lesions in different parts of the brain.

The present generally accepted theory is that memory is divided into short-term memory and long-term memory. Some theorists prefer to use the term 'working memory' to 'short-term memory' – the difference depends on whether the **central executive**, which mentally manipulates the information, is included as part of memory. In practice, most people conflate the two terms. We will concentrate on the term 'working memory'. The term 'short-term memory' is useful as a reminder of timescale.

Recording the memory in the first place is called 'encoding'. Some theorists – for example, Anderson (2000) – consider that encoding takes place in a third memory, the 'sensory memory'. The sensory memory retains an exact copy of what is seen or heard (visual and auditory). It only lasts for a few seconds, possibly only 300 milliseconds. Some of this information is then passed on to the short-term memory/working memory where it is processed in some way and then sent to the long-term memory for storage.

Short-term/working memory is considered to consist of three components:

- a verbal short-term memory (store);
- a visuospatial short-term memory (store);
- a central executive where immediate mental processing of the information takes place. For example, with a mental arithmetic task, the numbers would be stored in the verbal short-term memory and manipulated in the central executive.

Once information has been lost from the short-term memory, no amount of 'remembering' will retrieve it – it is gone.

Long-term memory consists of two components: a non-declarative memory, which is unconscious, and a **declarative memory**, which is conscious – that is, you know that you are remembering.

The non-declarative memory contains:

- the **perceptual memory**, which stores representations of sensory experiences;
- the procedural memory, which stores skilled behaviour and actions that are usually acquired through extensive practice – for example, riding a bike.

The declarative memory contains:

- the semantic memory, which stores general knowledge about the world, language, categorical knowledge about concepts (familiarity);
- the episodic memory, which stores personally experienced events (recollection).

When we want to remember something, the information we need is brought back from long-term memory to short-term memory. This is called 'retrieval'.

If we have forgotten something, it could be due to problems with:

- recording the memory in the first place (encoding);
- the storing of the memory (storage);
- recovering the memory from long-term memory (retrieval).

Table 1.1   Memory

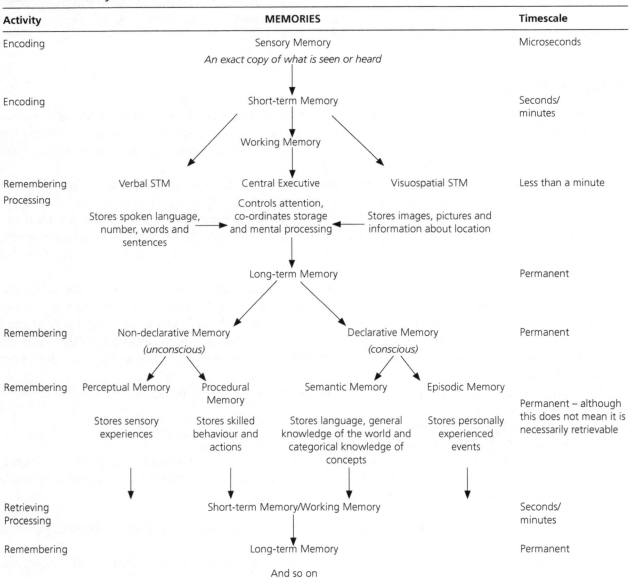

Activity	MEMORIES	Timescale
Encoding	Sensory Memory *An exact copy of what is seen or heard*	Microseconds
Encoding	Short-term Memory	Seconds/minutes
	Working Memory	
Remembering Processing	Verbal STM / Central Executive / Visuospatial STM Stores spoken language, number, words and sentences / Controls attention, co-ordinates storage and mental processing / Stores images, pictures and information about location	Less than a minute
	Long-term Memory	Permanent
Remembering	Non-declarative Memory *(unconscious)* / Declarative Memory *(conscious)*	Permanent
Remembering	Perceptual Memory / Procedural Memory / Semantic Memory / Episodic Memory Stores sensory experiences / Stores skilled behaviour and actions / Stores language, general knowledge of the world and categorical knowledge of concepts / Stores personally experienced events	Permanent – although this does not mean it is necessarily retrievable
Retrieving Processing	Short-term Memory/Working Memory	Seconds/minutes
Remembering	Long-term Memory	Permanent
	And so on	

Working memory, and severe and complex learning disabilities (SCLD)

Recent research has established close links between working memory skills and learning disabilities. Children who fail to make good progress in maths and literacy generally have a poor ability to store information over brief periods of time. This research has focused on children with moderate or specific learning disabilities (such as dyslexia or dysgraphia), comparing them with neurotypical children.

In the absence of formal research, we have designed our own experiment. A common learning task in our classrooms is to send a child to collect something. This requires him/her to remember what it is s/he is to collect. This task is rehearsed by carrying a tray with a symbol on it to, for example, the kitchen drawer to collect a spoon, a much practised task linking into procedural memory. Generally, we find that we can teach the child to collect a spoon supported by a symbol, but when we withdraw the support, even within the familiar context of needing the spoon to stir his/her cooking, s/he cannot remember that it is a spoon s/he needs when s/he reaches the kitchen drawer.

As children mature, their working memory usually becomes more efficient. One strategy that is known to improve this efficiency is rehearsal. Thus, the verbal short-term memory consists of two elements: a store and a rehearsal process. On its own, the store process decays in about two seconds; rehearsal (the act of mentally repeating the information) extends the memory, but to be effective has to be accomplished within two seconds. Typically, children do not rehearse until they are 7 or 8 years old. People with severe learning disabilities do not reach such a developmental age, so they probably do not have this rehearsal option.

Children with severe and complex learning disabilities process information slowly. An impaired working memory could explain why these children find it so difficult to learn to understand and use verbal language; they simply cannot remember a word long enough for it to get into their long-term memory. In our experience, our learners tend to rely on their visuospatial short-term memory. If we present information visually, we have a lot more success in terms of our pupil's apparent understanding. Hence, the use of **object of reference**, symbols and sign language for communication (see pp. 51 and 55).

Last, there is plenty of research that describes executive dysfunction as a core deficit of autism (Boucher et al., 2008: 76). **Executive function** is an umbrella term used to describe a collection of brain functions that include working memory, planning, initiation and monitoring of action, impulse control and mental flexibility. Recently, new technologies of brain imaging have been able to offer insights into the way people with an ASD think (Just et al., 2007). The theory is that normal brain functioning consists of a collaboration between different cortices (areas) of the brain. This collaboration is described as 'connectivity'. The new technologies imaging suggests that in autism this collaboration is loosened or underfunctioning, and that this functional underconnectivity is a general characteristic of the autistic brain and is the root cause of all their difficulties. This underconnectivity theory fits well with previous theorising about autism – for example, Frith's Weak Central Coherence Theory and Baron-Cohen's **Theory of Mind** – and is further developed under the heading of mouse models later in this chapter.

Weak central coherence is based on an understanding of how information processing typically occurs. Most individuals can recall the gist of an interaction or occurrence. Individuals with ASD often focus on the details and this can be at the expense of understanding the bigger picture.

Most of our pupils have a diagnosis on the autistic spectrum and we suspect that this is part of a trend to diagnose more children with severe learning disabilities with the condition. Eighteen years ago, when Lindy started working at St Crispin's School, very few children were diagnosed with an ASD; now there are very few children who are not, particularly by the time they reach the secondary school. This is probably just part of a general trend of increased diagnosis of previously missed cases (Keen and Ward, 2004).

Without an efficient working memory, the learner has to be provided with supports – **scaffolding** – to enable him/her to engage in learning. Supports come in a variety of forms:

- Physical support, practising what is to be learnt with hand-over-hand support, gradually withdrawn, but reinstated again when necessary as a prompt.
- Visual supports, using initially photos, then symbols and then symbol sentences to remind the learner what the task is.
- Gestural supports, pointing at objects and positions, and indicating gesturally the task in hand.
- Verbal supports, using speech to support the activity.

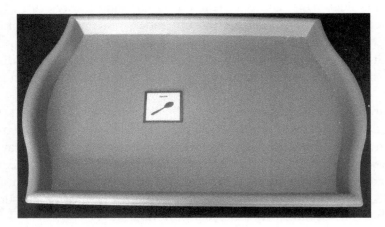

Figure 1.1   A symbol support

In a **Total Communication Environment** (see p. 51), all four supports are frequently employed simultaneously.

The working memory also feeds into the long-term memory. If a child has a working memory deficit, then less information gets to the long-term memory, so less information has been learnt.

Results of impaired working memory skills

Gathercole and Alloway (2008) describe four main warning signs of working memory failure:

- Incomplete recall, in which the learner forgets some or all of the information required to complete the task.
- Failure to follow instructions, in which the learner cannot remember the instructions.
- Place-keeping errors, in which the learner cannot remember what it is they have done and what comes next.
- Task abandonment, which is the most common, in which the learner gives up. Teachers often interpret this behaviour as not concentrating or not trying or being easily distracted.

These signs are further complicated with learners with communication problems (all children with severe learning disabilities have communication problems; East and Evans, 2006: 62) by the fact that it is difficult to know whether you have presented the information to the learner in a way in which they can understand in the first place.

Long-term memory and severe and complex learning disabilities

Boucher et al. (2008) use comparisons with adults with memory problems acquired by trauma to suggest that children with an autistic spectrum disorder and severe and complex learning disabilities have a developmental form of global amnesic syndrome caused by brain damage, which results in an impairment of the declarative memory.

This developmental damage to the declarative memory is the main cause of both the language impairment and the impairment of verbal intelligence, and thus of overall intellectual disability. Language acquisition is affected first and then intellectual ability because concepts normally acquired via language would be cumulatively affected by the consequent delay in language acquisition.

The theory makes a distinction between children with an ASD and SCLD with or without some speech. They suggest that complete or near complete absence of language results from total or near total loss of declarative memory; but where there is some understanding and use of verbal language, then the declarative memory is less damaged (Boucher et al., 2008: 275).

The non-declarative memory is relatively spared from damage. Non-declarative memory is sufficient for learning based on activity and sensory experiences. Implicit learning can be achieved based around daily living skills and routines. Visuospatial abilities are also relatively spared of damage.

Boucher et al. compare children with an autistic spectrum disorder and severe and complex learning disabilities to children with an ASD, and no or few learning disabilities, and suggest that it is this wide-scale damage to the declarative memory that makes the difference to their ability range. It seems logical to suggest that the disabilities that children with SCLD but not an ASD have with learning could be due to damage to the declarative memory.

This does not imply that we do not try to teach children with SCLD to understand and use spoken language. A declarative memory is not something that can be easily measured, so we cannot know how much declarative memory exists. It implies that we should understand why the children find so many difficulties in learning and offer them appropriate levels of support and teaching styles.

The results of an impaired declarative memory

Semantic memory

- Difficulties in understanding language.
- Difficulties in using language.
- Difficulties in forming concepts.
- Difficulties in remembering facts and knowledge.

Episodic memory

- Difficulties remembering things that have happened to them or things they have done.

It is important to remember that the procedural memory is usually undamaged and that this memory can be used for a lot of learning – for example, how to do things like bake a cake or get to places like the bus stop.

Mouse models

Another area of autism brain research uses mouse models (Crawley, 2012). An example of this research is in studies of disorders resulting in learning disabilities, which are caused by a single gene, that include features of autism – for example, **Rett syndrome,** fragile X syndrome, tuberous sclerosis and **Angelman syndrome**. When an affected gene is known, researchers can alter or remove this gene in a mouse and track its effect. Although the genes are different in each case, researchers look for results in common.

The results of this research focus on nerve cells (the brain has around 100 billion nerve cells called 'neurons') and the various impairments caused by the different genes. Nerve cells have branches called 'dendrites' and 'axons'. Dendrites bring information to the cell and axons take information away from the cell. Information from one nerve cell transfers to another across a 'synapse'.

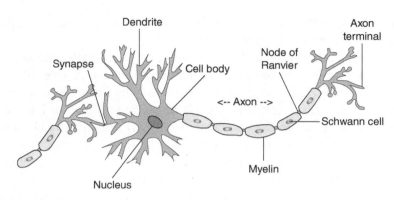

Figure 1.2   Nerve cell

In Rett syndrome, the affected gene causes nerve cells to develop fewer synapses and the synapses that do develop are dysfunctional. These synapses make weak connections which tend to fail (this failure causes the regression that is typical of Rett syndrome). In fragile X syndrome, the dendrites grow wildly and produce too many spines, again causing problems. In Angelman syndrome, the synapses are impaired and fail to join the nerve cells together effectively. In tuberous sclerosis, the axon bundles which travel from one brain region to another are muddled and abnormal. Sometimes more than one problem occurs at the same time – for example, mice with Rett syndrome and fragile X syndrome also have problems with their synapses.

The theory is that autism, which has no singular genetic cause, could be a disorder of brain connectivity, that there are either too many or too few synapses and that these synapses may be too weak or in the wrong place. Additionally, communication between two types of brain cells – excitatory and inhibitory – is unbalanced; there are too many inhibitory brain cells and this prevents learning from taking place. These results have been found in Down's syndrome mice as well.

Research with Rett syndrome mice investigating degenerative vision has identified critical periods of brain development (Bilimoria, n.d.: 8). It is very difficult to alter genes; but there are prescription drugs that change the excitatory/inhibitory balance in the brain, which may be able to be used during these critical periods to help brain circuits develop more normally (Crawley, 2012).

These learners have significant underlying problems with learning and these problems have to be respected. They are not being lazy, difficult or unmotivated. It is not a case of finding the right carrot. They have genuine difficulties with engaging in learning. Teachers have to observe their learners very carefully and assess what they can learn, and how best they can be supported to learn. Since learning is limited, reasoned choices have to be made about what exactly to teach them. They cannot afford to waste time; they have to concentrate on essential knowledge and skills. This does not mean just life skills.

Other causes of memory problems

Stress and memory

Stress affects both the storage and recall of memory. If a child is stressed at the time of learning, it is less likely they will remember the learning; and if the child is stressed when trying to recall information, they are less likely to remember it. Sadly, children with severe and complex learning disabilities are frequently stressed; indeed, one could say frequently very stressed, due mainly, but not solely, to their lack of communication, they do not understand what is happening and they cannot do anything about this. Sometimes this stress is short-lived, but sometimes it continues for weeks or months and may be linked to a psychiatric disorder or pain. It may also be linked to external factors such as moving house/school or changing circumstances at home – for example, parental divorce or a new baby, or sadly something as simple as a change of school taxi.

Sometimes, stress is caused by more deep-seated psychiatric problems. It can be difficult to recognise the symptoms of psychiatric disorder in children with severe and complex learning disabilities; nevertheless, psychiatric disorders are extremely common in this group. Around 36 per cent of children with learning disabilities suffer from psychiatric disorders, compared to 8 per cent of children without learning disabilities; this prevalence is particularly marked for children with an ASD (Emerson and Baines, 2010: 3).

Short-term stress affects the learning at that point, but long-term stress can cause regression across the whole learning profile of the child. Regression is a fact of life with children with severe and complex learning disabilities; it happens, and teachers have to work out what learning has been retained and proceed from that point. Parents, in particular, can find this regression very difficult. *Learning Tracks* can track regression; untracked, it just seems that the child is failing to meet their targets. Sometimes, regression can be solved by finding exactly what caused the problem and dealing with it.

Case Study

Last year, Andrew suddenly exhibited massive regression. His ability to process communication and to communicate regressed; toileting regressed; his ability to feed himself and drink appropriately was lost – he would put too much food and drink in his mouth and make himself sick. He was extremely stressed and upset all the time.

His parents, doctor and teaching team searched and searched for what the problem could be ... It turned out to be in-growing toenails. Once his toenails were removed, he returned to his normal sunny self. He had no way of telling us that he had a problem with his toenails, which were obviously causing him considerable pain; indeed, he probably did not know himself the source of his pain. He did not indicate in any way that his toes were the problem. This episode lasted 18 months – a very significant period of time.

Andrew's behaviour and learning are very closely linked to his health, and he has frequent colds and ear infections when everything regresses. This health-related short-term regression is very common in our school. It is unrealistic to expect the child to engage in new learning at these times and efforts should be put into maintenance of learning (see Maslow's hierarchy of needs, p. 68).

Epilepsy

The prevalence rate of epilepsy among people with learning disabilities has been reported as at least twenty times higher than for the general population (Emerson and Baines, 2010: 3). Most classes at our school have children with epilepsy. Epilepsy causes learning and memory problems in two main ways:

- During the learning, children can experience different partial seizures which result in absences of different kinds, which means that the child has been mentally absent from the learning experience.
- Other types of seizures can simply wipe out memories. A series of severe seizures can wipe out a lot of memory and therefore cause regression.

A child with epilepsy may have a very uneven learning record. Sadly, children with epilepsy can be quite unwell. Unwell children find learning difficult.

Conclusions

Children with severe and complex disabilities have significant disabilities with memory, particularly their working and declarative memories. They need teaching styles that support these disabilities.

It is very important that their teachers know what they know and understand, and track that they are maintaining this knowledge; indeed, a significant part of their school day may need to be assigned to practising and maintaining knowledge.

Teachers need to plan to use the procedural memory for learning, which is an active learning style. The children need to be involved in doing things; they cannot be taught by 'chalk and talk'. What children know one day will not necessarily be what they know another day. Teachers need to be flexible enough to deal with this – that is the nature of teaching in a school for children with SCLD. There will need to be a lot of supported repetition of activities.

Despite a teacher's best-laid plans, children may not learn the lessons that are prepared for them and this can be very disheartening for a teacher. Teachers have to understand that this is no one's fault – not theirs, nor the child's – and concentrate their energies on maximising what can be learnt and in being inventive in the ways that learning opportunities are presented.

References

Anderson, J.R. (2000). *Learning and Memory: An Integrated Approach*. New York: John Wiley & Sons.

Boucher, J., Mayes, A. and Bigham, S. (2008) Memory, language and intellectual ability in low-functioning autism. In Boucher, J. and Bowler, D. (eds) *Memory in Autism*. New York: Cambridge University Press.

Bilimoria, P. (n.d.) Breaking into the autistic brain. Boston Children's Hospital (www.childrenshospital.org/news-and-events/research-and-innovation-features/breaking-into-the-autistic-brain).

Crawley, J. (2012) Translational animal models of autism and neurodevelopmental disorders. *Dialogues in Neuroscience*, 14(3): 293–305.

East, V. and Evans, L. (2006) *At a Glance: A Practical Guide to Children's Special Needs* (2nd edn). London: Continuum International Publishing Group.

Emerson, E. and Baines, S. (2010) Health inequalities and people with learning disabilities in the UK (www.improving healthandlives.org.uk/uploads/doc/vid_7479_IHaL2010–3HealthInequality2010.pdf, accessed 21 May 2015).

Gathercole, S.E. and Alloway, T.P. (2008) *Working Memory and Learning: A Practical Guide for Teachers*. London: Sage.

Just, M.A., Cherkassky, V.L., Keller, T.A., Kana, R.K. and Minshew, N.J. (2007) Functional and anatomical cortical under-connectivity in autism: Evidence from an fMRI study of an executive function task and corpus callosum morphometry. *Cerebral Cortex*, 17(4): 951–61.

Keen, D. and Ward, S. (2004) Autism spectrum disorder: A child population profile. *Autism*, 8(1): 39–48.

2

Learning and Teaching Theories

Some theories of learning are direct bases for *Learning Tracks*; others have influenced our thinking in the development. The first theory is that learning is based on prior learning. Educational theorists who espoused this concept include Dewey (1859–1952), Skinner (1904–1990) and Vygotsky (1896–1934).

It is often difficult to find out what children with severe and complex learning disabilities know and understand. In our experience, at the end of the school year, when it is time to discuss a child's learning with their next teacher, teachers are very good at communicating essential facts like obsessions and triggers, health needs, communication needs and behavioural issues but find it very hard to communicate adequately what they know and can do. We believe that a teacher needs to understand what their pupils know and can do in order to plan and implement further learning. This is particularly important for children who find learning difficult, as they are generally unable to make adjustments to different teachers and teaching styles that more able children can and do on a regular basis. *Learning Tracks* was designed to facilitate communication of what the child can do and hopefully then what they understand and support planning for subsequent learning.

There is a range of learning theories which underpins a range of learning and teaching styles. In most classrooms, more than one teaching style is employed, and a classroom for children with severe and complex learning disabilities is no different in this respect; the teacher has to choose which particular style is appropriate for each experience. Learning theories are generally divided into behaviourist, cognitive and social theories, although there can be considerable overlaps.

Behaviourism

Behaviourism is a theory of learning based on the idea that all behaviours are acquired through conditioning. Conditioning occurs through a reaction to a stimulus. Behaviourists consider that it is our responses to stimuli that form our behaviours and that evidence of learning is a change in behaviour. Pavlov (1849–1936) was the father of behaviourism and experimented on dogs.

Classical conditioning is a term that Pavlov used to describe learning that occurs when an unconditioned stimulus – for example, a dog salivating when he is given food – is paired with a conditioned stimulus – for example, a bell being rung just before the dog is given food. After much repetition, this results in a conditioned response – i.e. the dog salivating when he hears a bell ring. Classic conditioning sees the learner as a passive recipient of knowledge (Gray and MacBlain, 2012: 30–2).

Skinner (1904–1990) believed that learning was an active process, and developed the theory of *operant conditioning* in which learning occurs when behaviour is either rewarded or punished. Positive reinforcement such as praise, ticks, stars or chocolate strengthens behaviour, and negative reinforcement such as a cross, a telling off or the naughty step discourages behaviour (Gray and MacBlain, 2012: 36).

Skinner's principles for the promotion of effective learning were:

- Present the information in small steps.
- Give rapid feedback on the learning.
- Let pupils learn at their own pace.

In the 1950s, Skinner worked on computer-assisted learning (CAL), in which children worked through carefully designed programs of learning at their own pace. These learning programs gave frequent feedback.

Behaviourism was the principal educational theory in schools in the UK until the 1960s, underpinning rote learning (learning by heart) and frequent testing (such as spelling tests every Friday morning). It is still very much in evidence in education. The following are some examples of this theory:

- The **Individualised Educational Programme (IEP)** or **Education, Health and Care Plan (EHC)**, which is designed for the individual child (principle 3) and in which the targets are often written – for example, Paul will … – and other such target-setting.
- Star charts, stickers, time on the computer and other rewards.
- Naughty step, withdrawal from pleasant activities, detention and other such deterrents.
- Frequent testing.
- Some computer learning programs.
- Behaviour modification.
- **Applied Behavioural Analysis (ABA)**.
- **Task analysis**, in which tasks are analysed and broken down into small sequential steps, and planned for teaching in a correct sequence enabling the learner to learn the first step and the move on to the next step and eventually be able to perform the complete task.

Task analysis has been used in the development of *Learning Tracks*.

Task analysis is particularly useful for learning where the component parts have a reasonably natural order, so that the first part can be taught first and so on. We find it useful for teaching such skills as dressing. So, when helping a child learn to undress, we start by pulling items off hands and feet and then move on to encouraging the child to take their arms out of their coat. This is an area that is not generally taught in initial teacher training as typically developing children can usually undress themselves when they come to school, although some still require help with dressing (see H10).

Cognitive theories: constructivism

Cognitive theories of learning emphasise a learner's active construction of understanding. Piaget (1896–1980) considered that knowledge is constructed by the learner based on the interaction of experience and thinking about the experience (Gray and MacBlain, 2012: 43). Bruner (1915–) also viewed learning as something that the learner is actively engaged in and promoted learning by discovery. Both theorists have promoted active learning (Gray and MacBlain, 2012: 105).

Active learning

Active learning does have a variety of interpretations. At the simplest level, it is learning by doing, by engaging in activity. This is the type of learning that children with SCLD do best, using mainly their procedural memory to remember learning. These children do not learn by listening to explanations; they do not understand the language. They have to be shown what they must do and then be guided through the learning.

Vygotsky (1896–1934), another constructivist, coined the term 'zone of proximal development', which is the distance between what the child can do independently and what he can do with a 'more knowledgeable other's' (an adult's or a more experienced peer's) support. He used the word 'scaffolding' to describe the act of providing a child or young person with the appropriate assistance that would enable them to achieve a task. Once the child or young person masters the task with support, the scaffolding can be removed and they will be able to complete the task independently (Gray and MacBlain, 2012: 69).

The philosophy underpinning *Learning Tracks* is that appropriate learning experiences/activities are planned for, along with the level of scaffolding required. The scaffolding is then removed in gradual phases at a pace determined by the child or young person. This provides success, and progression is recorded across challenge, breadth and application. In the experiential phase, responses are fully supported. In the contextual phase, responses are supported by a range of prompting, routine and context. In the generalised phase, responses begin to be spontaneous and independent.

The following case study describes support at experiential and contextual phases.

Case Study

Using symbols at snack scaffolding at an experiential phase

Two adults and one child. One adult is the communicative partner who does all the communicating with the child. The other adult sits behind the child and is the physical prompter and facilitates but does *not* communicate. Resources: crisps and crisp symbol.

The Communicative Partner (CP) presents the favoured snack (usually crisps) and entices the child with it.

Child reaches out for crisp. The Physical Prompter (PP) takes the child's hand, places it on a symbol and helps the child to hand the symbol over.

PP gives the child a crisp and says 'crisps'.

This is repeated at least 15 times in one session.

Yes, we know that crisps are not healthy food, and we have tried all sorts. The advantages of crisps are that: 1) they are desirable, and this does not work unless the child really wants what is on offer; and 2) they can be broken up into very small bits (allowing for plenty of practice) and it still works as well.

Using symbols at snack scaffolding at a contextual phase

Two adults and four children in a groupwork situation around a table. One adult, the Communicative Partner, and the other, the Physical Prompter, for all the children.

Resources: the CP has a choice of three snack items on plates, each with a symbol in front of it and each child has the symbols for these items on the front of their Picture Exchange Communication System (PECS) folder.

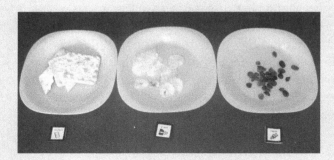

Figure 2.1   PECS and snack items

(Continued)

(Continued)

Everybody sings and signs the time for snack song. CP then names and shows the children the three snack items and their symbols and sits expectantly.

Child 1 chooses a symbol of a breadstick and hands it over to the CP, who then says 'breadstick' and hands her a piece of breadstick.

Child 2 is clearly struggling. CP entices the child with a favoured item (we always know the favoured items). Child 2 picks up a carrot symbol (not a favoured item) and gives it to CP. CP says 'carrot' and gives Child 2 a carrot. Child 2 flings carrot. CP then holds the crisp symbol next to the crisps and holds out her hand. PP scaffolds by putting Child 2's hand on the crisps symbol. Child 2 picks up the crisps symbol and hands it over and so on, and everybody is happy.

Both Vygotsky and Bruner emphasise the role of language in learning as part of the formation of generalised knowledge and although children with SCLD do generalise some learning, much of their learning stays firmly tied to specific contexts.

Developmental Learning Theory

This theory was first developed by Piaget who believed that as a child learns s/he passes through an invariant series of stages and substages. These stages are a universal developmental pathway through which all children pass in the same order. Piaget called the stages:

- Sensorimotor (0–2 years).
- Preoperational (2–7 years) – further divided into the preconceptual phase (2–4 years) and intuitive stage (4–7 years).
- Concrete operational stage (7–11 years old).
- Formal operational stage (11–15 years old).

Various aspects of Piaget's work have been both criticised and developed by other theorists such as Donaldson (1978: 30) and Hughes (1986: 12). Nevertheless, his work is hugely influential in the education and care of young children. His ideas are the basis of child **development charts** which are universally used to check on 'normal' development. These charts are based on hours of observation of normally developing children, leading to lists of typical behaviours in different areas of development for different age groups.

Much research suggests that children and young people with learning disabilities show the same sequence of development as those without disabilities, but that development for children with learning disabilities is characterised by regression and oscillation. Children and young people may indicate one level of reasoning in relation to a task, yet, when completing the task at a later date, perform at a lower level. Additionally, children and young people with severe learning disabilities may show different levels of ability in response to different tasks and materials; they will have a spiky profile. Of our case study children, Dougal shows the most spiky profile; he is more able numerically than would be expected by the rest of his profile.

Bruner described his theory of learning development through three stages of representation. Each stage is a way in which information or knowledge is stored and encoded in memory. The stages are generally sequential, although not necessarily age-related like Piagetian theories. Going through the stages is essential to truly understanding the concept.

Bruner's stages of representation

1. Enactive (action-based).

The concrete stage: this stage involves learning by doing. Bruner believed that learning starts with an action, touching, feeling and manipulating (definitely using the procedural memory).

2. Iconic (image-based).

The pictorial stage: this stage involves images to represent physical learning of the first stage. This can be done by drawing images of the objects on paper or by picturing them in one's head or manipulating photos or **Boardmaker symbols** (still using the procedural memory but moving to use declarative memory as well in terms of episodic and semantic memories).

3. Symbolic (language-based).

The abstract stage: the last stage involving using images from the second stage and representing them as words and symbols. The use of words and symbols enables concept development (using the declarative memory).

We have categorised different phases of learning in *Learning Tracks* as:

- Experiential phase: learning prior to the development of mental representations (pre-symbolic and pre-language – broadly comparative to Piaget's sensorimotor stage).
- Contextual phase: learning at an early symbolic stage supported by familiar contexts and prompting (broadly comparative to Piaget's preconceptual stage early in his preoperational stage).
- Generalised phase: learning using language and learnt concepts across a range of contexts.

Bruner's stages of representation have influenced *Learning Tracks* in that the stages of learning are also broadly comparative to *Learning Tracks* phases of learning:

- The enactive stage and experiential phase are broadly the same involving the idea that the learners learn by actively/physically doing things.
- The contextual phase is influenced by the iconic stage in that children with SCLD do not usually draw, but at this level their learning experiences are significantly supported by the use of Boardmaker-type symbols and/or photos which they may manipulate themselves as part of the learning. The pupils in our school are predominantly visual learners. It is generally accepted that both people with an ASD (Shield, 1999: 52) and those with Down's syndrome (Down's Syndrome Educational International) favour visual learning.
- The symbolic stage and generalised phase are also broadly the same.

We expect learners to develop through these phases in the order described. We also expect learners to be learning different lessons in different phases at the same time; a learner might be in an experiential phase for 'making choices' but in a contextual phase for communicating 'no'. Lastly, the third phase is where generalisation and concept formation takes place, using the declarative memory.

We have included a development chart in *Learning Tracks*. We recommend using this to get a feeling for the approximate level of learning at which a learner is functioning (see the online accompanying booklet: *Learning Tracks*).

Bloom's taxonomy

Bloom's taxonomy was created in 1956 under the leadership of educational psychologist Dr Benjamin Bloom in order to promote higher forms of thinking in education, such as analysing and evaluating rather than just remembering facts (i.e. rote learning). It is a way of describing how a learner's performance develops from simple to more complex levels in their affective, psychomotor and cognitive domains of learning. The most commonly referred to part of the taxonomy is the cognitive domain (Bloom et al., 1956).

In the cognitive domain, there were six stages: knowledge, comprehension, application, analysis, synthesis and evaluation. In 2001, Anderson revised these six stages to remembering, understanding, applying, analysing, evaluating and creating.

The problem with this from the point of view of a teacher at a school for children and young people with SCLD is that it starts with remembering, and although pupils clearly use memories, they are not usually the memories of facts, rules and concepts (semantic memory) that mainstream school learning tends to be based on. We have described in the memory section the problems that our children and young people have with remembering. We needed more stages to enable us to evidence the small steps of learning that our children and young people engage in. Claire Marvin developed the framework below to assess the small steps that children with profound and multiple learning difficulties make, and we felt it could easily be adapted to our needs (Marvin, 1998: 126).

Experience and achievement

Encounter: being present during an experience.

Awareness: noticing that something is going on.

Response: showing surprise, dissatisfaction, enjoyment.

Engagement: directed attention, focused looking and/or listening, showing interest, recognition or recall.

Participation: sharing, turn taking, anticipation, supported involvement.

Involvement: active participation, reaching out, joining in, doing, commenting.

Attainment: gaining, consolidating, practising skill, knowledge, concepts and understanding.

(Adapted from Brown, 1996)

We sorted the responses with reference to the three phases of learning – experiential, contextual and generalised. Encountering, noticing and responding are included in experiential learning; engaging, participating and communicating are included in contextual learning; and remembering, understanding and applying are included in generalised learning.

Table 2.1   Framework for recognising achievement

Response	Descriptor
Encounter (encountering)	Learners are present during an activity.
Awareness (noticing)	Learners appear to show awareness that something has happened and notice, or they fleetingly focus on an object/person.
Response (responding)	Learners attend and begin to respond to what is happening, often inconsistently. They begin to distinguish between people, objects, events, places.
Engagement (engaging)	Learners show more consistent attention to and can tell the difference between specific events, objects, people, etc.
Participation (participating)	Learners begin to share, take turns and anticipate familiar sequences of events (possibly with support).
Involvement (communicating)	Learners reach out, join in, 'comment' on activity and actions/responses of others.
Gaining skills and understanding (remembering, understanding, applying)	Pupils gain, strengthen or make general use of their skills, knowledge, concepts or understanding that relate to their experience of the curriculum.

Adapted from Qualifications and Curriculum Group, Welsh Government, *Routes for Learning* (2006).

█ Experiential learning   ⊠ Contextual learning   ⠿ Generalised learning

Generalised learning is where this framework for learning overlaps with Bloom's revised taxonomy. We extended Bloom's taxonomy to cover experiential (solid grey) and contextual learning (cross-hatch).

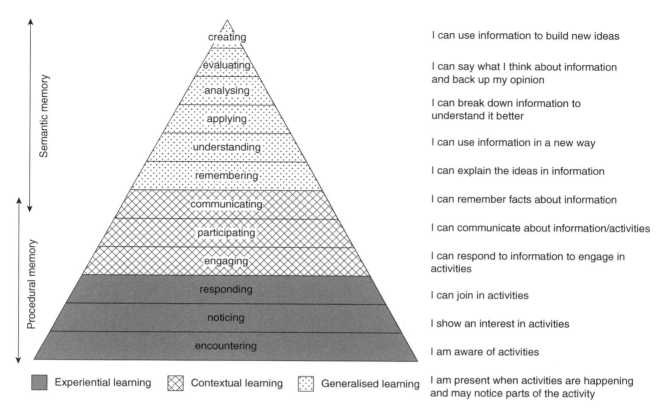

Figure 2.2 **Bloom's taxonomy – extended diagram**

Developed by Lindy Furby and Jilly Catlow, St Crispin's School, Edinburgh. Adapted from Brown, E. (1996) cited in Marvin, C. (1998) Teaching and Learning for Children with Profound and Multiple Learning Difficulties. In Lacey P. and Ouvry C. (eds) (1998) *People with Profound and Multiple Learning Difficulties: A Collaborative Approach to Meeting Complex Needs*. London: David Fulton, p. 126.

These responses became the level descriptors for *Learning Tracks*.

Table 2.2 **Level descriptor chart**

	Experiential		Contextual		Generalised
	Responding Noticing Responding		Engaging Participating Communicating		Remembering Understanding Applying

These level descriptors are used to track each child's progress on learning outcomes. By tracking the children and young people's learning experiences, progress can be planned to move through the levels of learning or planned for a broader range of experiences at the same level. Teachers can use the tracking descriptors when planning learning outcomes to link planning documents (for example, IEPs) with the tracking document; for more details, see Chapter 3 'Standards and Expectations', and Chapter 7 'The Framework for Recognising Achievement'.

When we decided to share *Learning Tracks*, we felt that it was necessary to make adjustments for the English curriculum, so we have matched our descriptors to the P levels.

Social theories

Vygotsky (1896–1934) was a social constructivist. He believed that social interaction is the basis of cognitive development and that everything a child learns is achieved on two levels: first, at a social level (interpsychological) and then at an individual level (intrapsychological). A child learns by interacting with others and then internalising this learning. He thought that prior to the age of two, children were influenced primarily by biological forces, but after that all higher forms of learning originate in interactions with the people around them. He called this social

Table 2.3 P levels chart

Response	Descriptor	P level
Encounter (encountering)	Learners are present during an activity.	P1 (i) Pupils encounter activities and experiences: • They may be passive or resistant. • They may show simple reflex responses (e.g. being startled at sudden noises or movements). • Any participation is fully prompted.
Awareness (noticing)	Learners appear to show awareness that something has happened and notice, or they fleetingly focus on an object/person.	P1 (ii) Pupils show emerging awareness of activities and experiences: • They may have periods when they appear alert and ready to focus their attention on certain people, events, objects or parts of objects (e.g. attending briefly to interactions with a familiar person). • They may give intermittent reactions (e.g. sometimes becoming excited in the midst of social activity).
Response (responding)	Learners attend and begin to respond to what is happening, often inconsistently. They begin to distinguish between people, objects, events, places.	P2 (i) Pupils begin to respond consistently to familiar people, events and objects: • They react to new activities and experiences (for example, withholding their attention). • They begin to show interest in people, events and objects (e.g. smiling at familiar people). • They accept and engage in coactive exploration (e.g. focusing their attention on sensory aspects of stories or rhymes when prompted).
Engagement (engaging)	Learners show more consistent attention to and can tell the difference between specific events, objects, people, etc.	P2 (ii) Pupils begin to be proactive in their interactions: • They communicate consistent preferences and affective responses (e.g. reaching out to a favourite person). • They recognise familiar people, events and objects (e.g. vocalising or gesturing in a particular way in response to a favourite visitor). • They perform actions, often by trial and improvement, and they remember learned responses over short periods of time (e.g. showing pleasure each time a particular puppet character appears in a poem dramatised with sensory cues). • They cooperate with shared exploration and supported participation (e.g. taking turns in interactions with a familiar person, imitating actions and facial expressions).
Participation (participating)	Learners begin to share, take turns and anticipate familiar sequences of events (possibly with support).	P3 (i) Pupils begin to communicate intentionally: • They seek attention through eye contact, gesture or action. • They request events or activities (e.g. pointing to key objects or people). • They participate in shared activities with less support. They maintain concentration for short periods. • They explore materials in increasingly complex ways (e.g. reaching out and feeling for objects as tactile cues to events). • They observe the results of their own actions with interest (e.g. listening to their own vocalisations). • They remember learned responses over more extended periods (e.g. following the sequence of a familiar daily routine and responding appropriately).

(Continued)

(Continued)

Response	Descriptor	P level
Involvement (communicating)	Learners reach out, join in, 'comment' on activity and actions/responses of others.	**P3 (ii)** Pupils use emerging conventional communication: • They greet known people and may initiate interactions and activities (e.g. prompting another person to join in with an interactive sequence). • They can remember learned responses over increasing periods of time and may anticipate known events (e.g. pre-empting sounds or actions in familiar poems). • They may respond to options and choices with actions or gestures (e.g. by nodding or shaking their heads). • They actively explore objects and events for more extended periods (e.g. turning the pages in a book shared with another person). • They apply potential solutions systematically to problems (e.g. bringing an object to an adult in order to request a new activity).
Gaining skills and understanding (remembering)	Learners can remember facts about information.	**Speaking** **P4** Pupils repeat, copy and imitate between 10 and 50 single words, signs or phrases or use a repertoire of objects of reference or symbols: • They use single words, signs and symbols for familiar objects (e.g. cup, biscuit), and to communicate about events and feelings (e.g. likes and dislikes).
Gaining skills and understanding (understanding)	Learners can explain ideas in information.	**P5** Pupils combine two key ideas or concepts: • They combine single words, signs or symbols to communicate meaning to a range of listeners (e.g., 'Mummy gone' or 'More drink'). • They make attempts to repair misunderstandings without changing the words used (e.g. by repeating a word with a different intonation or facial expression). • Pupils use a vocabulary of over 50 words. **P6** Pupils initiate and maintain short conversations using their preferred medium of communication: • They ask simple questions to obtain information (e.g., 'Where's the cat?'). • They can use prepositions, such as 'in' or 'on', and pronouns, such as 'my' or 'it', correctly.
Gaining skills and understanding (applying)	Learners can use information in a new way.	**P7** Pupils use phrases with up to three key words, signs or symbols to communicate simple ideas, events or stories to others (e.g., 'I want big chocolate muffin'): • They use regular plurals correctly. • They communicate ideas about present, past and future events and experiences, using simple phrases and statements (e.g., 'We going cinema on Friday'). • They contribute appropriately one-to-one and in small group discussions and role play. • They use the conjunction 'and' to link ideas or add new information beyond what is asked. **P8** They link up to four key words, signs or symbols in communicating about their own experiences or in telling familiar stories, both in groups and one-to-one (e.g., 'The hairy giant shouted at Finn'). • They use an extensive vocabulary to convey meaning to the listener. • They can use possessives (e.g., 'Johnny's coat'). • They take part in role play with confidence. • They use conjunctions that suggest cause (e.g., 'because' to link ideas).

Experiential learning   Contextual learning   Generalised learning

network 'a social matrix'. He described 'tools' such as speech and writing which people use to mediate their environments, and believed that children initially use these tools to communicate needs and that the internalisation of these tools leads to learning (Gray and MacBlain, 2012: 70). Difficulties with social interaction and communication are two of the main criteria for a diagnosis of an autistic spectrum disorder, and these difficulties have a pervasive effect on all aspects of learning and behaviour.

Bandura (1925–) believes that children learn from other people through observation, imitation and modelling. He describes the people the learner observes as models and the models provide behaviour that can be imitated. He describes a famous experiment in which children were shown a film of a woman hitting a doll; when the children were left in a room with the same doll, they hit it – they had learnt by observation (Gray and MacBlain, 2012: 97).

Much learning in our school comes about through supported imitation because the pupils' understanding of language is so limited that they cannot be told what to do.

Case Study

Hand group lead by our occupational therapist

Our occupational therapist (OT) leads the children though a range of exercises designed to improve their hand–eye co-ordination and motor control. She sits on one side of the table showing the children what they are to do. It is the role of the other adults to help the children imitate the actions. So the OT takes some playdough and rolls it out into a sausage shape. The teacher supporters help the children to flatten their hands, and then push and pull the hands backwards and forwards to help make the sausage shapes. Five sausages are made and then the song *Five Fat Sausages* is sung and acted out. Our pupils do like singing or listening to familiar songs. Songs are great motivators.

Jean Lave has developed the theory of Situated Learning, in which learning is unintentional and based on real-life activities in everyday cultural contexts as opposed to classroom learning, which tends to be abstract and out of context. She calls this 'unintentional learning: legitimate peripheral participation'. She considers that learning inside and outside school progresses through collaborative social interaction (Lave and Wenger, 1991). We use a lot of real-life activities for learning.

Theories about autism and learning

Some 40 per cent of children with an ASD/C (autistic spectrum disorder/condition) have severe learning disabilities; a high proportion of children with severe learning disabilities have a diagnosis on the autistic spectrum; these imply that classrooms with children with severe and complex learning disabilities have a high proportion of children with an ASD. In our school, a high proportion of children have a diagnosis on the autistic spectrum. The philosophy, theory and content of *Learning Tracks* is heavily influenced by theories of autism and learning.

What is an autistic spectrum disorder/condition?

Autistic spectrum disorder is a complex developmental disability. It is diagnosed by observation of behaviours matched to a set of criteria. Lorna Wing (1928–2014) and Judith Gould developed a set of criteria that are known as the 'Triad of Impairments' which are the basis of most criteria used to diagnose autism.

Triad of impairments

Impairment of social interaction: ranging from completely cut off and aloof and socially passive, through active but odd, to displaying over-formal social behaviour.

Impairment of social communication: ranging from a complete lack of formal communication (no speech or signing, etc.), through only expressing own needs, or using echolalic and repetitive speech, or only very factual and literal speech, to simply being pedantic.

Impairment of imagination and thought: ranging from an inability to play imaginatively with toys and other children, engaging in stereotypical activities, having a restricted set of interests and activities, to difficulties understanding abstract concepts such as feelings and emotions. (Wing and Gould, 1979)

To complicate matters further, many children with an ASD (and children with learning difficulties) also have sensory problems. These can be hypersensitivity or hyposensitivity. Hypersensitivity is being over-sensitive to stimuli, when the child seeks to avoid sensory experiences, seen in covering ears, refusing to enter the music room, averting eyes, or refusing to eat anything but particular bland foods. Hyposensitivity is being under-sensitive to stimuli, when the child seeks heightened sensory experiences seen in head banging, flickering fingers in front of eyes, rocking and biting themselves. Some children can suffer from both hypo- and hyper-sensitivity at different times (Wong, 2009).

So, if you take the criteria for an ASD, add sensory problems and then the memory of a child with severe learning disabilities, you have a very complex individual indeed. You might be forgiven for thinking that you cannot form relationships with 'these children' and that it is impossible to teach 'these children'. However, our experiences and the experiences of many teachers refute this. Despite their social and communication difficulties, relationships are formed, and these relationships are rich and satisfying; despite the children's learning disabilities, learning is accomplished. Indeed, Rita Jordan (1997) considers that education is the most effective method for dealing with the difficulties associated with autism, and that education can remediate the effects of autism (not cure it) and improve the quality of life for people throughout their whole life.

Comorbidity of Down's syndrome and ASD

Some 5–7 per cent of children with Down's syndrome are likely to be diagnosed with ASD as well (Capone, 1999). Comorbidity of Down's syndrome and ASD is a complex combination. Down's syndrome can be diagnosed easily, but it often takes a while to realise that ASD is also present. Children with Down's syndrome and an ASD are clearly distinguishable from children with just Down's syndrome and SLD. Children with Down's syndrome and ASD are usually less impaired in social relatedness than children with just ASD. NZDSA (2004) suggests that there are four key markers that suggest an ASD in a child with Down's syndrome:

- Extreme autistic aloneness.
- Anxiously obsessive desire for the preservation of sameness.
- Lack of eye contact.
- Repetitive stereotypical behaviour.

Parents suggest that in their experience it is better to consider autism as the primary disability and use the strategies and therapies that you would use for ASD.

Attachment disorder

John Bowlby (1907–1990) developed a theory about the relationship between a primary caregiver and an infant – termed an 'attachment relationship'. He believed that this relationship affected all the child's subsequent relationships. He theorised that a child who is not securely attached to his/her primary caregiver would have difficulties making and keeping relationships (Keenan and Evans, 2009: 249–56). Some theorists consider that extreme disturbance of this attachment relationship results in 'attachment disorder'. Children with attachment disorder display some of the following symptoms:

- Poor eye contact.
- Poor impulse control.
- Poor peer relationships.
- Inappropriately demanding and clingy behaviour.
- Indiscriminate affection with strangers.
- A lack of ability to give and receive affection.
- Violence towards self and others. (Martin, 2003: 255)

Attention Deficit Hyperactivity Disorder (ADHD)

ADHD involves inattention and/or hyperactivity and an impulsiveness that occurs more often and more severely than can be accounted for by the developmental age of the child (Keenan and Evans, 2009: 332). Many children with SCLD are inattentive to the tasks they are asked to engage in and are hyperactive and impulsive; much of this behaviour can be explained by their notional developmental age and their other disabilities. Some of these children are diagnosed with ADHD, usually when they are *very* hyperactive, and some of these pupils are on medication.

Engagement theory

The Complex Learning Difficulties and Disabilities Research Project have developed an engagement profile and scale. They consider that sustainable learning can only happen when there is meaningful engagement. Children with SCLD can be difficult to engage in learning activities. This scale can help teachers to assess children who do not currently engage in learning activities to analyse what they do engage in and what does motivate them. When working with children with SCLD we have to start where they are, with what engages them – hence, all the activities mentioned in the above paragraph. The scale also helps teachers to reflect on how individuals engage and increase this engagement.

Happiness theories

Unhappy children cannot learn effectively. There is a lot of research on emotions and learning. Basically, positive emotions can enhance learning and negative emotions block learning. Children with SCLD often have many reasons to be unhappy:

- They do not understand what is going on.
- They don't know when (if ever) what is going on will end.
- They don't know where they are going or what is going to happen.
- The place they are in is too noisy, too bright, too smelly, the chairs are too hard.
- They want to do something else.
- Something they like or like doing is taken away and they don't know if or when they will get it back again.
- Something hurts but they don't know how to communicate this.
- They need something but cannot communicate it.
- They are frightened of somebody/something.

Daniel Goleman (1996: 6) believes that happiness inhibits negative feelings and increases available energies, thus calming negative thinking, giving the learner a rest from worrying and panicking, and a readiness and enthusiasm to engage in the task in hand. Since the late 1990s, there has been a great deal of interest in education in the concept of emotional literacy, and this is reflected in the Curriculum for Excellence in Health and Wellbeing for example:

HWB 0–01a/1–01a: 'I am aware of and able to express my feelings and am developing the ability to talk about them' (see H1).

Learning Tracks incorporates these learning outcomes. Emotional literacy is the ability to recognise, understand and appropriately express our emotions, and schools are increasingly becoming aware that this is an important area of the curriculum. It is a big area of learning for children with SCLD who clearly experience powerful emotions and need a lot of help to recognise, name and control these emotions. We will return to this in Chapter 5 'Health and Wellbeing'.

However, happiness theory is a step back from this. It is the idea that because children learn best when they are happy, it is incumbent on special needs teachers to help their pupils to be happy at school. Happiness is something that teachers can help make happen.

The influence of happiness theory is evident in *Learning Tracks* in the content of the learning experiences; they include experiences based on the activities that our children and young people enjoy doing. The absolute essential learning needs of children with SCLDs are communication and socialisation. These are best learnt in activities they enjoy doing – **intensive interaction**, rough-and-tumble play, circle activities like action songs, Forest School, cooking, snack, playtime – which are the contexts mentioned in *Learning Tracks*. It is also one of the things that make teaching children and young people with severe and complex learning disabilities enjoyable; to be effective, the teachers have to be happy, too – they also have to have fun. All the activities mentioned are also fun for the teacher. Teachers in special needs classrooms have fun!

References

Anderson, L.W. and Krathwohl, D.R. (eds) (2001) *A Taxonomy for Learning, Teaching, and Assessing: A Revision of Bloom's Taxonomy of Educational Objectives* (complete edn). New York: Longman.

Bloom, B., Englehart, M,D., Furst, E.J., Hill, W.H. and Krathwohl, D. (1956) *Taxonomy of Educational Objectives Handbook 1*. New York: Longmans.

Brown, E. (1996) *Religious Education for All*. London: David Fulton Publishers.

Capone, G. (1999) Down syndrome autistic spectrum disorder. Special Issue, *Disability Solutions*, 3 (5 and 6).

The Complex Learning Difficulties and Disabilities Research Project. Special school/early years engagement profile and scale (http://complexld.ssatrust.org.uk/uploads/CLDD%20research%20project%20%28Final%29%20Exec%20sum.pdf, accessed 21 May 2015).

Donaldson, M. (1978) *Children's Minds*. London: Fontana/Croom Helm.

Down's syndrome educational international. Development and learning (www.dseinternational.org/en-us/about-down-syndrome/development/, accessed 21 May 2015).

Goleman, D. (1996) *Emotional Intelligence: Why it Can Matter More than IQ*. St Ives: Bloomsbury Publishing.

Gray, C. and MacBlain, S. (2012) *Learning Theories in Childhood*. London: Sage.

Hughes, M. (1986) *Children and Number*. Oxford: Basil Blackwell.

Jordan, R. (1997) Education of children and young people with autism, France. *UNESCO Guides for Special Education, No 10: Special Needs Education*, Division of Basic Education (unesdoc.unesco.org/images/0011/001120/112089ev.pdf accessed 18 August 2014).

Keenan, T. and Evans, S. (2009) *An Introduction to Child Development*. London: Sage.

Lave, J. and Wenger, E. (1991) *Situated Learning: Legitimate Peripheral Participation*. Cambridge: University of Cambridge Press.

Martin, H. (2003) *Typical and Atypical Development*. Malden: Blackwell.

Marvin, C. (1998) Teaching and Learning for children with profound and multiple learning difficulties. In P. Lacey and C. Ouvray (eds) *People with Profound and Multiple Learning Disabilities: A Collaborative Approach to Meeting Complex Needs*. London: Andrew Fulton Publishers.

New Zealand Down Syndrome Association (NZDSA) (2004) DS-ASD Dual diagnosis Down syndrome and Autistic Spectrum Disorder. *Newsletter*, 25.

Qualifications and Curriculum Group (2006) *Routes for Learning: Additional Guidance*, Cardiff, Department for Education and Lifelong Learning, Welsh Government (http://learning.wales.gov.uk/docs/learningwales/publications/121113curriculumforlearnersen.pdf).

Shield, J. (1999) Daily living skills for young children. In Smeardon, L. (ed.) *The Autistic Spectrum Handbook 1999*. London: National Autistic Society.

Wing, L. and Gould, J. (1979) Severe impairments of social interaction and associated abnormalities in children: Epidemiology and classification. *Journal of Autism and Childhood Schizophrenia*, 9: 11–29.

Wong, C. (2009) Hyposensitivity and autism. *New Autism – Breakthrough Treatments for Autism* (www.newautism.com/hyposensitivity-and-autism/501/, accessed 21 May 2015).

Standards and Expectations

3

In Scotland, the national curriculum is statutory and is called the 'Curriculum for Excellence'. It commenced implementation in 2010, and is designed for all children and young people from the ages of 3 to 18. It provides young people with the skills, knowledge and attributes they need for learning, life and work in the twenty-first century. It is an inclusive curriculum, for all children. It contains the totality of experiences and outcomes which are planned for children and young people through their education, wherever they are being educated.

In 2004 and amended in 2009, the Education (Additional Support for Learning) (Scotland) Act introduced a new framework for providing for children and young people who require some additional help with their learning. **Co-ordinated Support Plans (CSP)** became the main planning mechanism for teaching children and young people with additional support needs. A Co-ordinated Support Plan is a statutory plan prepared by the education authority when a child or young person requires significant additional support from the education authority and from at least one other agency from outwith education in order to benefit from school education (Scottish Government, 2010). The plan lists skills, capabilities and the needs of the child, then sets out the educational objectives to be achieved by each individual. A few children with SCLD might not have a CSP due to the support offered by their school (such as speech and language therapy); generally, they would have an Individualised Educational Programme (IEP) (non-statutory), which, in educational terms, is very similar in planning experiences and outcomes.

The National Curriculum in England (2014) is also statutory and contains programmes of study and attainment targets for all subjects at all key stages for most maintained schools. However, in England, there is a particular set of Attainment Targets (P scales) designed for children with special educational needs who cannot access the National Curriculum.

In England, the **Special Educational Needs and Disability (SEND)** code of practice became law in September 2014. The code of practice required schools and institutions to keep clear records of the special educational needs that an individual child or young person has, the provision put into place to support them and the outcomes expected to be achieved. For children with SCLD, this will nearly always be as part of an Education, Health and Care Plan (EHC). In the EHC plan, there are two sections that are particularly pertinent in teaching and learning:

- Summary of Skills and Strengths, Needs and Supports: this leads to the next section.
- Outcomes and Provision: this section of the EHC plan sets out the Special Education Provision for the pupil and the arrangements for monitoring the plan.

SEND is clear that schools need a robust recording system for children's learning. In England, there is a formal reporting system for English, Mathematics and Science.

The other major change is that local authorities must ensure that parents, children and young people are involved in all the decision-making, including planning outcomes and how these outcomes are to be met (Nasen, 2015). This is true of both England and Scotland. *Learning Tracks* can be brought to meetings to help inform parents of progress, and discuss further experiences and outcomes. Involving children with SCLD in decision-making about their learning is difficult and really means that parents and teachers need to be aware of what they would like or choose if they could understand the decision-making process – that is, knowing the child. EHCs, IEPs and CSPs actually all follow much the same format once you get to that part of planning learning, which is basically listing strengths, needs and learning outcomes. Both the Scottish and English systems state that they favour SMART targets (Education Scotland, 2013; DfEE, 2001).

SMART targets are Specific, Measurable, Achievable and Realistic, and set against an appropriate timescale. SMART targets, in special education, tended to be very behaviourist and extremely specific. For example, a SMART target might be as follows:

> Calum will match the three symbols – lunch, circle and playtime – correctly to symbols on a matching board three times a week with an 80 per cent accuracy, by June 2016.

Definitely specific, measurable, probably achievable, probably realistic and in a timescale – but one wonders about the quality of learning? Symbols need to be learnt in real-life settings to develop real-life meaning and use.

Penny Lacey has developed a concept of 'scruffy targets' – targets that are Student-led, Creative, Relevant, Unspecified, Fun for Youngsters – which are based on a process of strengths and needs analysis, and as far as possible are student-led. The teacher lists the pupil's strengths, then their needs, and then what the pupil needs in order to move learning on.

So, in this case, Calum is showing an interest in symbols and recognises the snack symbol. Calum needs to extend his recognition/use of symbols.

Alternative learning outcome:

> Calum will notice the lunch symbol on the way to lunch, the playtime symbol on the way to play and the circle symbol on the way to circle.

It is student-led in that Calum is showing an interest in symbols. It is definitely relevant and it can be fun. It could be unspecific if it was felt appropriate not to actually name the symbols to allow Calum to notice symbols which are important to him. Scruffy targets allow much more freedom for meaningful learning.

In practice, any exemplars given for learning outcomes tend to be more meaningful and less SMART – for instance, the Council for Disabled Children in their EHC plan examples suggest:

- To support Toby's responses to learning and play opportunities.
- Emma will develop her listening skills so that she is able to follow a simple spoken instruction given by a member of staff.

Using our own extended Bloom's taxonomy, we have developed a set of planning descriptors which, while not strictly SMART, offer teachers the ability to plan steps with appropriate levels of engagement and support. These planning descriptors are mapped to appropriate P levels:

> ... will encounter situations where ... (P 1i).
>
> ... will notice/be aware of ... (P 1ii).
>
> ... will respond to ... (P 2i).
>
> ... will engage in activities where ... (P 2ii).
>
> ... will participate in activities where ... (P 3.i).
>
> ... will communicate about ... (P 3.ii).

... will remember information/vocabulary/processes related to ... (P 4 and 5).

... will understand information/vocabulary/processes related to ... (P 6 and 7).

... will apply skills and knowledge related to ... (P 8).

▦ Experiential learning   ▧ Contextual learning   ⦂ Generalised learning

In the experiential phase (solid grey section), responses are fully supported. In the contextual phase (cross-hatched section), responses are supported by a range of routine and context. In the generalised phase (spotted section), responses are beginning to be spontaneous and independent. These are various levels of scaffolding. Children with SCLD need a lot of practice to retain their learning.

Children and young people can demonstrate progress in three ways:

1. By achieving breadth of learning through an increasingly wide range of experiences – for example: 'Calum will notice the swimming symbol on the way to swimming, the Forest School symbol on the way to Forest School and the soft play symbol on the way to soft play.'
2. Responding to the level of challenge by becoming increasingly independent – for example: 'Calum will respond to the lunch, circle and playtime symbols by moving towards that activity.'

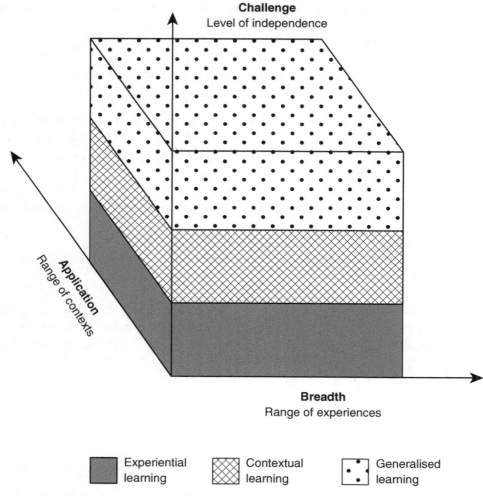

Children and young people can make progress in a range of ways.
They can demonstrate their progress by:

- achieving a **breadth** of learning through an increasingly wide range of experiences
- responding to the level of **challenge** by becoming increasingly independent
- **applying** what they have learned in a range of contexts

Challenge
Level of independence

Application
Range of contexts

Breadth
Range of experiences

▦ Experiential learning   ▧ Contextual learning   ⦂ Generalised learning

Developed by Lindy Furby and Jilly Catlow, St Crispin's School, Edinburgh. Adapted from Education Scotland, Standards and Expectations (2013).

Figure 3.1   Standards and expectations

3. Applying what they have learnt in a range of contexts – for example: 'Calum will notice symbols in art, music and gym.'

So, once an outcome is achieved, there are many possibilities for planning another target at the same level, or making a very small step on to the next level – for example, the step between noticing and responding while still maintaining challenge, high expectations and aspirations. Children with SCLD find these small steps very challenging.

The main difference between the English and Scottish SEN systems is curricular content. *Learning Tracks* is a tracking booklet for the Curriculum for Excellence. How we designed this document is discussed in Part 2 'The Curricular Content of *Learning Tracks*'. The Curriculum for Excellence lists Experiences and Outcomes, which we have elaborated and then added tracking descriptors. The English P levels do not list experiences and outcomes but describe the different performance indicators at each level in each area of the curriculum: 'these performance descriptors can be used as non-statutory guidelines describing some of the types and range of performance that pupils with SEN who cannot access the National Curriculum might characteristically demonstrate' (DfEE, 2014). These performance indicators are very similar to, and can be mapped to, our tracking descriptors.

Learning Tracks then lists the experiences and outcomes that children and young people with SCLD need to engage in at school to gain the skills, knowledge and attributes they require for learning, life and work in the twenty-first century. These experiences and outcomes are as relevant to children in England as they are to children in Scotland and can be reported at the appropriate P levels because that is how they are charted. The structure of *Learning Tracks* supports teachers to maintain high standards and high expectations of their pupils.

SEND is very clear about the teacher's responsibilities. They should:

- ensure that decisions are informed by the insights of parents and those of children and young people themselves (share *Learning Tracks* at meetings);
- have high ambitions and set stretching targets for them (use *Learning Tracks* to set targets, see Part 3);
- track their progress towards these goals (*Learning Tracks*);
- keep under review the additional or different provision that is made for them;
- promote positive outcomes in the wider areas of personal and social development (*Learning Tracks* has a whole section on Health and Wellbeing);
- ensure that the approaches used are based on the best possible evidence and are having the required impact on progress (DfE and DH, 2014), see Part 2.

References

Council for Disabled Children (December 2013) Coordinated Assessment and EHC plan. Appendix 1 CDC EHC Plan Checklist and Examples (www.sendpathfinder.co.uk/files/page/556885/Appendix_1_CDC_EHC_Plan_Checklist_and_Example_Plans.pdf, accessed 21 May 2015).

Department for Education (DfE) and Department of Health (DH) (2014) Special Educational Needs and Disability Code of Practice: 0 to 25 years. Statutory guidance for organisations who work with and support children and young people with special educational needs and disabilities (www.gov.uk/government/publications/send-code-of-practice-0-to-25, accessed 21 May 2015).

DfEE (2001) Supporting the Target Setting Process (revised March 2001). Guidance for effective target setting for pupils with special educational needs (http://webarchive.nationalarchives.gov.uk/20130401151715/http://www.education.gov.uk/publications/eOrderingDownload/DFEE-0065–2001.pdf, accessed 21 May 2015).

DfEE (July 2014) Performance – P Scale – Attainment Targets for Pupils with Special Educational Needs (www.gov.uk/government/uploads/system/uploads/attachment_data/file/329911/Performance_-_P_Scale_-_attainment_targets_for_pupils_with_special_educational_needs.pdf, accessed 21 May 2015)

Education Scotland (2013) CfE Briefing 13, Planning for Learning, Part 3: Individualised Educational Programmes (IEPs) (www.educationscotland.gov.uk/resources/c/genericresource_tcm4809983.asp, accessed 21 May 2015).

Lacey, P. (n.d.) Smart and Scruffy Targets (www.orchard.sandwell.sch.uk/mssn/SMART%20and%20SCRUFFY%20Targets.doc, accessed 5 October 2015).

Nasen (2015) Everybody included: The SEND code of practice explained (www.sendgateway.org.uk/download.everybody-included-the-send-code-of-practice-explained.html, accessed 21 May 2015).

Scottish Government (2010) Supporting Children's Learning Code of Practice (www.scotland.gov.uk/Resource/Doc/348208/0116022.pdf, accessed 21 May 2015).

PART 2

The Curricular Content of *Learning Tracks*

The curricular content of *Learning Tracks* is based on years of experience of working with children and young people with SCLD, and collaboration and advice from other professionals such as speech and language therapists (SLTs), occupational therapists (OTs), educational psychologists and clinical psychologists. The curricular content contains experiences and outcomes that teachers, speech and language therapists and occupational therapists feel are essential learning for children and young people with SCLD. *Learning Tracks* was designed for our school and therefore includes the learning experiences that we engage our children and young people in. In Part 2, we will describe some of the activities with a theoretical background of why we consider these activities are worth engaging in. In your school, you will probably engage in different activities and these can be inserted into the tracking booklet (see Part 3 'Adapting *Learning Tracks*'). We designed the experiences and outcomes in two ways:

1. We fitted essential learning experiences such as dressing skills into the Curriculum for Excellence experiences and outcomes.
2. We analysed the Curriculum for Excellence experiences and outcomes and designed or selected suitable activities that would lead to the successful achievement of these experiences and outcomes.

Learning Tracks is designed to be used to track and plan for small learning steps in Communication, Language and Literacy, Health and Wellbeing, and Mathematics. These are the three essential areas of the curriculum for children and young people with severe and complex learning disabilities across the globe and, although the document was based on the Scottish National Curriculum, it is fully transferable across the UK and beyond.

Communication, Language and Literacy is one of the areas of particular difficulty for learners with SCLD and affects everything else as it is essential for nearly all learning.

Health and Wellbeing incorporates many of the life skills necessary for young people to live as independent, content and healthy a life as possible.

Mathematics contains other essential life skills, such as matching, sorting, counting, measuring, telling the time and using money.

These areas equate to the three core subjects at Early Level in Curriculum for Excellence (Scotland) and to two of the three core areas of the English National Curriculum – English and Mathematics, plus one of the foundation areas, Personal Social and Health Education (PSHE) and citizenship. Personal, Social and Health Education is contained in the Health and Wellbeing section.

We have matched the tracking to Early Level (Scotland) and P scale attainment targets for pupils with special educational needs (England).

Both Scotland and England have national curricula – broad curricula that entitle our young people to a wide range of experiences. It is expected that all children will experience the full range of the curricula and, for the most part, these experiences are recorded in some other format. There simply is not enough time in the day to track all learning in the detail of *Learning Tracks*.

It is, nevertheless, essential to track this learning in detail because these are the essential areas of learning for children and young people with SCLD. In order to plan further learning, it is essential to know:

- what a learner can do;
- what is secure;
- what needs practice.

It is important to be able to track *small* steps in learning because these small steps are significant achievements and very important to the learner, their parents and their teachers, and from one such small step, another small step can be planned. These small steps are appropriate, ambitious and challenging targets for these learners. It is also important to track regression in order to remediate, otherwise inappropriate targets could be set. *Learning Tracks* can provide a history of learning to interested others (e.g. Ofsted or Education Scotland) in a way that is difficult to see in IEPs, CSPs and EHCs.

Learning Tracks also records learning that might be outwith any targets set that year; learning that may be based on previous targets, or learning that is part of the school curriculum but is not a particular target for the year. It is important to track this learning because it can be the basis of new targets but also because some very significant learning goes on outside particular planned targets. Lastly, it is important to track this learning because it gives a fuller picture of a child's knowledge and skills.

Learning Tracks can show a learner's spikes (learning they are good at) and troughs (learning they find difficult). It is important to support learning that is found difficult, but it is also important to enable further learning in areas of success.

In this part of the book, we will describe approaches which will build up a **prosthetic environment** (Lindsley, 1964) for people with SCLD. A 'prosthetic environment' replaces 'missing parts' with artificial structures. Elements of this prosthetic environment are:

- alternative communication systems, usually using symbols replacing spoken language;
- visual timetables, replacing a global understanding of life;
- strategies/rules for living, replacing social understanding and knowledge.

Reference to *Learning Tracks* will be made throughout this book using heading codes – for example, C4, which means Communication, Language and Literacy, 4th set of experiences and outcomes. Thus, particular experiences and outcomes can be searched for online.

Communication, Language and Literacy

4

Teaching children who have severe communication deficits to understand and use language has a profound impact on their lives and those of all who interact with them (Goldstein, 2002: 20). It really is the most important thing we can do.

Severe and complex learning disabilities actually covers a wide range of communication abilities, from children with no formal communication skills, to children who can understand and speak a little speech/signing/communication with symbols, to children who might seem to have a lot of speech but on closer study much of it is echolalic (echoing other's speech, often from well-watched films) and often not used for communication.

What is communication?

Communication is the successful sharing of ideas and feelings. Usually, we think of this as spoken conversation between people, but it is actually more than that. We also use facial expressions, gestures and body language all the time. Using these we give each other important messages, often without knowing it. Communication has two complementary facets: receptive (receiving and understanding) and expressive (making an idea, or feeling known).

Most people learn to communicate as they grow from a baby to an adult. However, if that development is slowed down or interrupted, a child may not learn about:

- watching people when they are talking;
- listening to people when they are talking;
- the meaning of words; or
- how to have a conversation.

What happens when communication does not develop as expected?

The child can't understand what people are saying to him/her and s/he has no way of telling people what s/he wants or feels – the world is a very scary place.

S/he can have massive tantrums because:

- s/he needs something – but can't tell anyone what it is;
- s/he doesn't want to have or do something – but doesn't know how to tell anyone;
- s/he doesn't know what is going to happen next;

- s/he doesn't know where s/he is going;
- s/he doesn't know where his/her mum/dad/favourite carer is going and if they are ever going to come back.

S/he can simply decide that it is all too difficult and withdraw into his/her own world and become very passive.

S/he can become very attached to routines because s/he does not know what is going to happen next and is very likely to hate having her/his nice safe routines disrupted.

Children without a good communication system are often frightened and frustrated. The only thing they have left to communicate with is their behaviour. The more frightened and frustrated they are, the more likely it is that the behaviour will be challenging behaviour – biting, hitting, kicking and having tantrums.

This behaviour is communication. Sometimes their teachers, parents, brothers and sisters and friends know exactly what it is they want or don't want. Very often they don't know. This can be very frustrating for everybody. Sometimes, even though it is known what they want, it can't always be given it to them, but neither can they be made to understand the reason why.

It is *really important* that children learn an effective form of communication.

There are a variety of interventions used to help children with severe and complex learning disabilities learn to communicate, some of which we will discuss below.

Total Communication Environment

'Total Communication' is a term invented in 1967 by Roy Holcomb in California to describe a practice in deaf education that used of a variety of approaches to communication – signing, speech, gestures, and so on, concurrently. It was considered that the main benefit to the deaf child was that it kept open all modes of communication, enabling choice. The concept of a Total Communication Environment has been used by teachers of children with an ASD for several decades. When it started, it was mainly the use of both speech and signing to support language learning. Research then identified that teaching language skills to children with an ASD using both speech and signing was more effective than using just speech.

Total Communication has been developed to provide an environment for learning language that includes using gestures, symbols, photos, writing and object signifiers – in fact, every single possible means of communication concurrently, although possibly not all at the same time.

At our school, we have a Total Communication Environment involving using many forms of communication all at the same time:

1. To enable the children to choose to learn and understand at least one.
2. To support one form – for example, speech – by another form – for example, symbols.

Our Total Communication Environment involves speech, signing, objects of reference, gestures, photos, symbols and the written word.

We chose to use a Total Communication Environment because:

- All the pupils have some problems with communication.
- Some pupils do not understand that the noises we make when we talk have meaning. They do not understand the purpose of speech.
- Some pupils understand that when we talk we mean something, but they don't know what it is we mean.
- Some pupils understand and say many words, but get confused when lots of words are put together in sentences.
- All our pupils, whatever their level of understanding, have much greater problems understanding communication when they are under stress, and at these times they need more support.

- All people are better at learning in one way than another. Some like to listen, some prefer to see things and some learn best by doing things. In general, our pupils prefer to learn by looking at things. Indeed, many of our pupils have a particular strength in learning by watching.
- Listening to speech and working out what it means at the same time can be quite hard. Spoken words are said and then they disappear – you have to remember them and work out what they mean. This is not always easy. Some of our pupils process the meaning of a word very slowly and so miss out on the whole sentence.
- Our learners need scaffolding to learn. We support speech with gestures, object signifiers, photos, signing, symbols and writing. We give visual support. Objects, photos and symbols remain visible and allow children the time to work out what they mean. We continue to use speech as well as signing and symbols because we do not know who will learn to speak or understand speech and who will not, and we always work towards the goal of children speaking if they can. However, the most urgent need is for each and every child in the school to have some system of communication that they can use.

The Total Communication Environment is an essential part of the teaching and learning of communication in our school and as such permeates *Learning Tracks* (C11).

Communication is receptive or expressive. Receptive communication is the ability to understand or comprehend communication. Expressive communication means being able to put thoughts into words and sentences. Generally, receptive communication is in advance of expressive communication. Both receptive and expressive communication are supported by a Total Communication Environment (see the chapter on 'Case Studies' for examples of understanding receptive and expressive communication).

Adults and speech

In a school for children with SCLD, it is very important to use simple language in short sentences or phrases, to talk slowly and clearly, and give the children time to work out what has been said and what it means. Sign the key words. Pause.

That is what we should do ideally. In practice, we all tend to talk too much, too quickly, using too many words, repeating ourselves, repeating ourselves using a new set of words that mean the same – for example, 'Stop playing and come to circle, put your toys down and come and sit over here.' Effectively, all the instructions mean the same, but in practice there are more words to understand.

It is very difficult for teachers, in particular, to stop talking, but we do try. The following are our rules for speaking to children.

General Rules for Speaking to the Children

1. Keep the language simple, clear and literal. Literal words are words that mean exactly what they say. Avoid expressions like: 'Don't *skip* the queue' 'Don't *barge* in.' Say: 'Go to the back of the queue, please.'
2. Speak slowly, and if you know them, sign the key words.
3. Try to avoid the word 'no', which can cause tantrums. Use words like 'stop' or, better still, instead of telling the child what not to do – for example, 'Stop drumming with your knife and fork' – tell him/her what s/he *must* do – for example, 'Put your knife and fork down, please.' It is always easier for a child to do something than to stop doing something. Also, children often just hear the last few words of a sentence, so the command 'Stop banging your fork, please' can be understood as 'Bang your fork please.'
4. A *pause* gives the child time to work out what it is you have said, what it means, and what you want them to do. Wait and then wait a little bit longer, and *then* wait a little bit longer. This is very difficult but it can be very effective.

5. If a child is having a tantrum, stop talking, or at the very least, say only the essential. When the children are under severe stress, they cannot understand what we say. Talking at children at times like these usually makes things worse.
6. Don't insist on eye contact. Some of our children can take in all the visual information they need with little sideways glances. Some of our children find keeping eye contact very distressing and the distress they feel gets in the way of understanding.

Elements of teaching/learning communication

There are a variety of well-researched approaches to teaching communication to people with SCLD – for example, Intensive Interaction, **Treatment and Education of Autistic and Related Communication Handicapped Children (TEACCH)**, PECS and Playboxes. Children with SCLD generally follow a similar sequence of development to children without disabilities. The very first steps of communication are learnt through play.

Early interaction/play (C3 and C10)

This is a *very important* stage and is the basis from which all further communication skills will develop. Early interaction involves joining in with someone else and having fun. Through playing and having fun with somebody else, a child learns to look at a person, to listen, to take turns, to copy and to join in with activities. Children learn to communicate through play. Some children with SCLD are quite difficult to play with, but this does not mean that it is acceptable to give up. Children at an early developmental level tend to enjoy rough-and-tumble play. This is a good starting point. Rough-and-tumble play can be used to encourage communication by:

• Stopping the play and waiting for any sign that the child would like it to continue.
• Imitating the child – joining in with the things s/he likes doing.
• Using simple repetitive language like: 'Ready, steady, go'; what happens if you leave off the word 'go' and wait?
• It is important that you enjoy the playing and laugh and be happy. It is important that we communicate to our children that they are fun to play with.

Autism and play

Play is enormously important for the development of social interaction and communication. Current general development theory states that **joint attention** (the co-ordinated attention between a child, another person and an object or event; Rutherford et al., 2007) is essential to the development of social communication skills in typically developing children. Impairments in joint attention in children with an ASD are well documented (Charman et al., 2003; Williams, 2008). A number of researchers have found that joint attention skills together with imitation skills predict later expressive language development in children with an ASD. Early language development is strongly linked to later academic achievement and social competence and is therefore one of the strongest predictors of positive long-term outcomes for people with an ASD. Joint attention and imitation are the bases of imaginative play. In the typically developing child they are learnt in the first year of life, starting with the synchronisation of movements and eye gaze, and turn-taking vocalisations between infant and carer. This synchronisation typically does not take place with infants with an ASD (Carpenter et al., 1998).

So, if joint attention and imitation are the foundations of social interaction and communication and these skills are learnt through play, then it would seem essential to engage children who lack these skills in playing. Difficulties in sharing imaginative play are included in the diagnostic criteria for autism and are described in the ***Diagnostic and Statistical Manual of Mental Disorder (DSM-IV)*** (American Psychiatric Association, 2000). Typically, children with an ASD are not motivated to communicate in order to share information and experiences. Koegel and Johnson (1989) suggest that the child's interests and preferences are used to tempt the child to communicate. As it is clear that motivation is the key to gaining and sustaining joint attention, using children's interests to encourage them to engage may increase their motivation to join in (Attwood, 1998). Engagement in interesting and enjoyable play with an adult facilitator who can introduce and develop symbolic and imaginative play can help develop joint attention and imitation. Strathclyde University has been leading a very successful project using playboxes to help develop symbolic play and joint attention (Marwick et al., 2013). Playboxes are used at our school to encourage joint attention and interaction.

Case Study

Playboxes

Structure: One adult and one child in a quiet safe space, two reasonably identical playboxes. The playboxes are pleasingly decorated boxes with lids; on the lid of one is a photo of the child and on the lid of the other a photo of the adult. Each playbox contains a blanket or piece of material, a teddy-like animal, bubbles and other hopefully motivating toys – for example, musical instruments, cars, bricks, animals, playdough, and pots and pans. Both child and adult have similar toys, the only exception being if one box contains a ball-run toy or skittles, the other box may contain the balls to encourage co-operation. Toys can be changed during the ten weeks if particular ones are found not to be motivating.

The playbox session lasts up to half an hour, depending on how long the child can stay involved. Each child has ten sessions, usually weekly. The play sessions are with a familiar adult (usually a nursery nurse or learning assistant) who knows the child well. Children's first sessions are very variable – for example, from one child yelling in a corner, to another child immediately curious, getting the toys out and happily experimenting and mouthing. The intention is to follow the child's lead, but if the child shows no interest, the adult may open her own box and play with her toys, or help the child hand-over-hand to open their box and get toys out.

A typical development is, for example, no interest, followed by solitary investigation of toys, parallel play (here the adult may copy the child's play and possibly copy and extend the child's play), to sharing toys and activities. The child often starts at a distance from the adult, comes closer and ends up sitting face to face. No pressure is put on the child at all.

Ellen

Ellen is 5 years old and has a **psycho-educational profile (PEP-R)** developmental age of 7 months. Ellen was immediately very sociable and happy banging, tapping and mouthing the objects in the box. After six weeks, she learnt to play with a cause-and-effect toy, purposefully making noises to cause it to perform and, by the end of the sessions, she had also learnt to play peekaboo. She thoroughly enjoyed every session, and particularly enjoyed the singing of songs and clapping to the songs.

Review

The staff involved in the playbox sessions enjoy them and feel that they help the children with joint attention and interaction. The staff encourage the children to use their new skills back in the classroom. Playboxes offer the children a calm unpressurised opportunity for individual attention at an appropriate level with a knowledgeable adult.

Intensive Interaction (C3)

People with SLCD and with or without an ASD can be very distant and difficult to reach, and are happiest on their own playing with little bits of string or crisp packets, not wanting to be with other people at all (see the chapter on 'Case Studies' for examples of individual special interests). They need to learn the very basics of communication; they need to feel comfortable with another person – indeed, to want to be with them and engage with them in some communicative behaviour.

Intensive Interaction is an empirically researched approach to the teaching of early communication and socialisation. Melanie Hind and Dave Hewitt developed Intensive Interaction in the 1980s while working at Harperbury Hospital School in England, with Gary Ephraim as the Principal Psychologist (Hind, 1999). Ephraim was surprised at the responses of people with SLD when he echoed back their sounds and movements. Almost every person sat up and took notice. Phoebe Caldwell (2006) points out that even people with SCLD in their fifties will recognise with interest their own sounds and actions. She considers that it is wired into the brain to do so.

Intensive Interaction is a method of teaching 'pre-speech fundamentals of communication' to people with SLD at a very early stage of communication development. It is based on mother-and-baby interactions where the mother responds to every sound/expression/movement the baby makes as if it has meaning and where the mother frequently echoes the baby's sounds, which confirms and gives value to the baby's utterings. This is how the first stages of socialisation and communication normally develop.

In practice, in schools, it consists of an adult working one-to-one with a child, concentrating all their efforts and energies exclusively on the child. It involves the adult observing the child very closely and responding to any sound, movement or facial expression the child makes as if it has meaning. Sometimes, adults copy the sound or movement, which usually gains the child's interest. Sometimes, the adult engages the child in activities known to please them, such as tickling or bouncing on a big ball. The idea is to build up a repertoire of early communication games based on what the child does or is interested in, in the same way that mums play peekaboo with their babies. Always the adult observes the child closely so as to move the interaction on in a way that is pleasing to the child. Once games have become familiar and desirable, the adult can 'withdraw' and wait for the child to initiate, and the communication dance can progress from there.

Below is an example of an Intensive Interaction game.

Peter was 7 years old, diagnosed with SCLD and ASD, and mainly pre-verbal (around five words, one of which was 'ball'). Peter really liked balls – both small balls and big balls. One of the Intensive Interaction games he loved was being bounced on a big ball in soft play. After a few weeks, I would bounce him until he was relaxed and happy and then stop. I would 'withdraw' – by that I mean go still and make my face impassive and wait, until Peter made some sort of noise to indicate he wanted more, then I would 'wake up', say 'Peter wants more' or even just 'more', and vigorously engage in the bouncing again. Fun for both of us. This would go on as long as I could physically maintain it, then we would have to move to a less physical game.

It is important that it is clearly fun for both participants, as an important part of Intensive Interaction is the learner learning that they are fun to be with and that other people are fun to be with as well. This playing also establishes early attention and engagement.

Intensive Interaction is the start of communication learning because we cannot teach anybody anything until we get their attention. There are other similar approaches to this learning: **responsive teaching**, the **Son-Rise** technique from America and **proximal communication**. The Son-Rise programme uses a special room for the play; indeed, our case study came from soft play, which is a special playroom. However, this style of working with children at an early stage of communication can be done spontaneously – for example, in the bus or in the playroom. It is a way of interacting with the child, just as a mother plays with her baby when changing his/her nappy; many one-to-one situations can be used profitably.

Making choices (C2)

Some of our pupils do not understand the purpose of communication. They do not understand what it is for. Others may understand but are simply not very interested in doing it. They prefer their own world.

A very basic understandable form of communication is asking for things you want. It is easy to understand the purpose of asking for things and the good thing is that you get a result, a reward. The reward may well motivate you into having another go.

One of our major starting points for making and communicating choices at school is snack. Most of our pupils like snack. For the purpose of helping children communicate, we have snacks they enjoy – usually crisps, biscuits and even sweeties – but if a child prefers grapes, we make these available. We break biscuits and crisps into small pieces so that the children have many opportunities to ask for a piece.

Throughout the school day we offer the children other choices using the same systems:

- They choose songs in circle.
- They choose toys they want to play with.
- They choose leisure activities.
- They choose food at lunchtime.
- They choose fitness machines in the fitness room.
- They choose ingredients in cookery.

Choice-making is tracked at C2.6 and 2.7 against all the different ways a young person can make their choices – using behaviour, body language, vocalisation, gesture, eye pointing, photos, symbol, sign, VOCA and speech. Nobody would be expected to work their way though all these different processes, but the way they do communicate throughout their school life can be mapped and *Learning Tracks* can be used to help a teacher decide on moving a learner on from one communication style to another – for example, from using pointing (gesture) to using a photo.

Situational understanding (C11)

We involve the children in routines. Every day we have circle, snack, playtime, lunch (to name but a few). We repeat and we repeat and we repeat. Gradually, the children begin to pick up clues about what is happening. They see the snack table being set up. They think 'snack' and when they are asked to, they sit down in their place. They do not necessarily understand the words, but they understand what is happening, the situation, and in time this will help them with understanding the words.

The children find these routines very reassuring. They can understand and anticipate what is happening. These experiences are repeated over and over again, day after day. It is the repetition that helps children to learn. Even the chairs where they sit are labelled with their photos, which is all very reassuring – they know where they have to be.

Timetables (M6 and H5)

As the children learn the different routines of the day, they are also introduced to timetables. The pupils can be very distressed when they do not know what is happening or what is going to happen. So, from the earliest days in school, we give them clear clues as to what they are going to do next.

All the children in the school have their timetables in a visual form.

Some children who are not yet ready to understand photographs or symbols have objects of reference to communicate what they are going to do next. An object of reference is meaningful for that particular child. Examples are:

- Holding out a Ball Pool ball means: 'We are going to soft play.'
- A plate means: 'It is time for lunch.'
- A booster seat means: 'We are going on the minibus.'

The next stage uses photographs of, for example, soft play, our lunch hall or Class 3's circle time. These are particular to each class.

The next stage uses Boardmaker symbols – a soft play symbol, a lunch symbol and a bus symbol. These symbols are used throughout the school, at home, at respite centres and in other schools and adult centres. The written words are printed above the symbol.

After that, the children may use a written word list. In one class, children may have different types of timetables according to what stage they are at. The actual timetables take a variety of forms:

- A vertical timetable with a pocket at the bottom to put finished activities in; the photos or symbols are fixed to the timetable with Velcro to make it easy to put them on and take them off (Figure 4.1).

Figure 4.1   A vertical timetable

- A horizontal timetable – often based on a ruler so that it can be carried around, which is used alongside a timetable, breaking down the current activity into smaller steps (Figure 4.2).

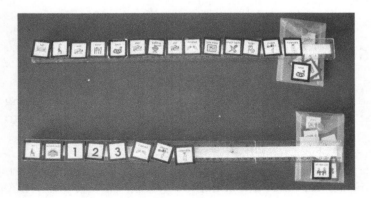

Figure 4.2   A horizontal timetable

- Small flip-chart type timetables which can be carried around (Figure 4.3).

Figure 4.3   Small flip-chart type timetables

- PECS: Picture Exchange Communication System.

Children with an ASD tend to be visual learners; indeed, most children with SCLD seem to find it easier to learn visual information. This may be due to the speed at which the brain can process visual information. Words are very ethereal; you say them and they disappear, which can be hopeless for the slow processor. Most schools now use symbols, pictures and photos to develop communication with children with SCLD. One can spend time with a picture; one can process it slowly and either refer to it or be referred back to it again should it be necessary. Pictures and symbols are used in a lot of different ways. A formal system of using symbols is PECS – Picture Exchange Communication System – which was developed from 1985 onwards by Andy Bondy and Lori Frost (2001). This is used in many schools, including our own.

The Picture Exchange Communication System is a communication system which starts by teaching a child to communicate with an adult by handing them a card with a picture on it. PECS is based on the idea that children who can't speak can learn to communicate using pictures.

Children use little cards with symbols on them to get things they would like, such as a crisps symbol card in exchange for crisps, or a bubbles symbol card for bubbles. Unlike speech, this can be physically scaffolded – an adult can aid a child hand-over-hand to pass the card over to the person with the desired object. The child learns that if they want a crisp and they hand over the crisps card, they will get one. Our case study Andrew has recently learnt this and he is finding it very empowering.

The most important things we are trying to develop with the picture exchange system are:

1. The idea that communication has a purpose (in this case, exchange of something for a desired object).
2. That communication is interaction with another person.
3. That it is possible to initiate or independently communicate without waiting to be asked. Many of our children don't communicate until asked 'What do you want?' and this relies on the adult knowing that the child wants something.

Some of our pupils have small sets of symbols for different situations such as snack. Some situations have special boards of symbols – for example, toys in the playroom, the fitness machines in the fitness room, musical instruments in the music room and a song board in a circle. Other children have a PECS folder which they carry between school and home with their own personal sets of symbols.

The children start with handing over one symbol to exchange for something and work up to handing over a whole sentence. When they hand over their sentence, they may speak or sign the sentence or just point to the symbols. This is developed by the child being taught more difficult skills such as using pictures to make whole sentences, to express preferences or to make comments.

PECS was originally designed to help non-verbal children with autism, but it is now used with adults and children with a wide range of diagnoses (including fragile X, **Down's**, **cri du chat**, Angelman and **Williams syndromes**, **cerebral palsy** and **developmental delay**) at an early stage of communication.

PECS is an essential part of the teaching and learning of communication in our school and as such permeates *Learning Tracks* (see C11). More information about PECS can be found at www. pecs-unitedkingdom.com/ (accessed 21 May 2015).

Literacy

This includes reading, writing, decoding and communicating with symbols, stories, factual scripts, drama and poetry.

Early emergent readers – who are beginning to grasp the basic concepts of book and print, and to acquire a command of the alphabet and develop phonological awareness skills such as recognising phonemes and rhyme – are typically at a developmental age of between 4 and 6 years. The pupils in our school, in common with most children and young people with SCLD, are typically at a notional developmental age of between 1 and 3 years, with a very few outliers reaching 4 years. Very few pupils learn to read and write in the conventional sense of the words. Out of our six case studies, only Dougal and Blair have basic reading skills, and Blair is a real outlier for the school. Donald is at a very early stage of learning to read.

This does not mean that we do not teach reading. It is well known that children with an ASD have spiky profiles and we do not know who will learn to read. Reading is a very important skill for people with an ASD and other learning difficulties, not just because it is a life skill but also because the written word is a great source for learning *about* language. If you are a slow processor, there is a lot of learning about language that most learners would get from listening to speech that is lost to you because of the transitory nature of speech – it is said and gone with the wind. The written word can be studied at leisure and returned to repeatedly and reflected on. This can be used in teaching to scaffold language learning. Owing to the very wide range of abilities in each class, most school-type learning such as reading, writing and mathematics is taught in individual **box work** or **workbox**. Box work is part of the TEACCH philosophy.

TEACCH is a programme designed to help people with an ASD live as independent a life as possible, including preparation for work. TEACCH was originally a child research project in the Department of Psychiatry in the School of Medicine, North Carolina University, USA, in 1966. Nowadays, practically every establishment with people with an ASD use some of their ideas, although it is unusual in the UK to adhere to the whole philosophy, which can be considered too behaviourist. TEACCH focuses on designing a supportive environment – for example, workstations and using visual supports, such as timetables and schedules to provide a visually structured framework to support understanding and reduce stress.

Our school uses timetables and schedules; we also use TEACCH workstations for individual one-to-one teaching and independent work.

Workstations

The workstations (Figure 4.4) are designed to minimise distraction. Ideally, they should have some soundproofing, but this is not possible so they consist of a table surrounded by screens.

The screens are blank except for work-related items such as timetables and schedules. When a child goes to the workstation, they know it is time for work. We use the workstation for two types of work: one-to-one teaching and independent work. Work is organised for both in boxes. The box full of work is put on the left and an empty box is put on the right. The child takes the work from

Figure 4.4   Workstation

the box on the left, does it and, when it is 'finished', puts it into the box on the left. When the left-hand box is empty, the work is finished and the child can go away or have their reward. In fact, there are many different individual organisations of the work:

- it may be folders;
- or several boxes;
- they may work from left to right;
- or from top to bottom.

However, they all have the same fundamental principle that the child is absolutely sure what work they have to do and absolutely sure when it is finished. People with an ASD often struggle when they do not know how long things are going to go on for.

Box work: one-to-one teaching

Any class has a very wide range of ability and the wide range is often spiky, particularly in the area of mathematics and literacy, so most mathematics and literacy teaching is carried out one-to-one, still working from boxes, and from left to right, but with an adult supporting or actively teaching the learning. The adult sits next to the learner, or opposite the learner, or very occasionally behind the learner, depending on the needs of the child.

Box work/workbox activities

Box work activities need to be relevant to a child's learning outcomes, visual, appealing and clear. There are many sites now which offer very good examples of workbox activities across the curriculum. Pinterest and Google Images, which lead you through to all sorts of websites, and TES Connect are all helpful places to look:

www.pinterest.com/karachambers/teacch-task-ideas/

www.google.co.uk/search?q=teacch+activities&es_sm=93&tbm=isch&tbo=u&source=univ&sa=X
&ei=_g9RVNzpCaTP7gaPi4HQBA&ved=0CCkQsAQ&biw=1283&bih=598

www.tes.co.uk/article.aspx?storyCode=6259180

www.shoeboxtasks.com/

(All accessed 21 May 2015)

Box work activities start with the youngest children with playful, engaging activities such as cause-and-effect toys. The aim is to engage their interest and participation.

Box work independent work

It is important that children and young people learn to work and play independently, and this can also be taught in a workstation. In this case, the activities are activities that the child likes and can do independently as the learning is independence. Frequently, a work schedule is also followed, so that the child is clear about the content and order of the work. Some children may need to work towards a reward, and this is also made clear.

Specific skills in literacy are taught in box work – for example, whole word recognition, phonics and reading-scheme books. One has to be very flexible when teaching children with SCLD and/or ASD to read. Some may respond to phonics.

Literacy Case Study

Blair

For many years, we taught Blair phonics in his box work and whereas he was very skilled at CVC words and other decoding skills, he showed no interest in phonics and seemed unable/unwilling to decode words when reading. So we gave up and decided to concentrate on teaching a functional vocabulary of whole words. Then, one day, a new photo appeared on his classroom door labelled with an unfamiliar name. Blair sounded it out. He now regularly uses phonics to decode new words in his reading.

Many children respond better to whole word learning and many will only learn motivating words or words that have purpose for them. For example, Colin, who despite our best efforts in encouraging him to read and his mum reading to him from six months, eventually basically taught himself to read and tell the time using the 24-hour clock, using the *TV Times* magazine from a desire to watch particular TV programmes. (He had absorbed learning from all our efforts, but nothing was used or apparent until he saw a purpose for everything.)

Reading can be developed from symbol sentences as all the symbols also contain text. It is also important to teach functional reading: reading to access recipes, shopping lists and toilets, for example. Due to the difficulties of motivating children with SCLD, very often the adults in the school make individual books to suit the interests of the children. *Learning Tracks* tracks the emergence of reading (C4).

Writing practice also occurs in box work and also along with other hand–eye co-ordination exercises in hand groups. *Learning Tracks* tracks the emergence of writing (C5).

The Communication, Language and Literacy section has an appendix which tracks common words. Schools can add charts for tracking sounds and phonemes if they wish.

Much of the reading is heavily supported by symbols and a great deal of literacy in the school depends on symbols. Whereas few children read words, many children read symbols, and symbols are used to label everything in school. Books are made about activities that have happened at school with both words and symbols; symbols are stuck on fact and fiction books.

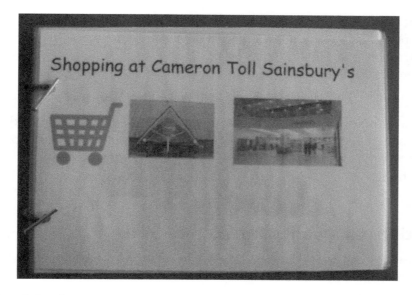

Figure 4.5   School-made books

Figure 4.6   A recipe using symbols

These books support the children's episodic memories because they are often about things that have happened to them. These books are very popular. Some children have Chat Books, which are home–school liaison books designed to promote discussion in which the child sticks photos and symbols of events at home and school to 'chat' about at school and home.

Activities which require following written instructions, such as a recipe, are 'read' with symbols (C3.13):

- Commenting activities are engaged in using symbols (C9).
- Questions are posed using symbols and answered using symbols (C7).
- Children use symbols and glue to 'write' (C4.3).
- Simple cloze procedure is engaged in with symbols (C8.2 and C8.7).

Literacy activities are engaged in on the interactive whiteboard and the computer using symbols where a mainstream school might use written words. Very few children learn to read using a reading scheme. Donald has had reading-scheme books in his box work, but he is now using school-made books. The stories in the reading-scheme books had become too complicated for him.

Communication, Language and Literacy Skills

Both the English and Scottish curriculums (and many others) are absolutely clear that *all* children should work towards skills in literacy.

One of the 'aims of the Curriculum for Excellence are that every child and young person should experience a traditionally broad Scottish curriculum that develops skills for learning, skills for life and skills for work, with a sustained focus on literacy and numeracy' (Donnelley, 2008: 8).

The National Curriculum for England aims to ensure that all pupils:

- read easily, fluently and with good understanding;
- write clearly, accurately and coherently, adapting their language and style in and for a range of contexts, purposes and audiences. (Statutory Guidance, 2014)

Communication, Language and Literacy skills have foundations on a myriad of earlier skills. We have incorporated a range of these earlier skills into *Learning Tracks*, listed with a range of supports (scaffolding).

Listening and talking (C3)

New teachers coming to work with pupils with SCLD can find it difficult to design learning objectives in listening and talking for pre-verbal or even pre-communicative children. The ability to listen and talk is based on an enormous range of pre-listening and talking skills which most children develop before they come to school. The challenge is to analyse the skills and list opportunities for learning these skills in a school situation, which is what we have tried to do in *Learning Tracks*. Listening and talking starts with the very basic beginnings – responding to stimuli (C3) – and develops through:

- Taking turns in Intensive Interaction with a list of typical Intensive Interactions.
- Attending to someone who is communicating with me, with a list of the skills involved in this, such as being aware of people, watching an adult's face and responding to greetings in a variety of circumstances.
- A list of essential 'words' that can be communicated – for example, 'yes', 'no', 'more/again', finished – broken down into how these words are communicated – behaviour, body language, vocalisation, … sign, VOCA, speech. Appendix 1 has a basic vocabulary list where a pupil's understanding and use can be charted.
- I can take my turn in simple circle and table-top games again with a list of skills contributing to this achievement – for example:
  - I can sit on a chair or supported seat appropriately ready to engage in a task:
    - with support;
    - without support.

- I can follow a simple instruction:

  ○ one information carrying word (ICW) symbol supported;
  ○ one ICW-signed support;
  ○ one ICW spoken;
  ○ one ICW text;
  ○ two ICW symbol supported, etc. ICWs are the essential elements of an instruction.

Information carrying words (Knowles and Masidlover, 1982)

One ICW

The child is presented with a selection of items or pictures – for example, a teddy, car, apple, cup, spoon. The adult says 'Find <u>teddy</u>' or, holding out their hand and looking expectantly, says 'Give me <u>apple</u>' without looking at the item or picture. (If the adult looks at the item, the child will follow their gaze.)

Figure 4.7   One ICW

Two ICWs

A selection of objects or pictures such as brush, cup, spoon is put on the table. A teddy and a doll are put out to act as contrasts. The adult gives the instruction:

- 'Give the <u>brush</u> to <u>teddy</u>.'
- 'Make <u>dolly</u> <u>jump</u>.'
- '<u>Brush</u> <u>teddy</u>'s hair.'

'Brush teddy's hair' still contains only two key words, because the assumption is that you wouldn't brush anything other than hair unless instructed.

- 'Give the <u>cup</u> to <u>dolly</u>.'

Figure 4.8   Two ICWs

(Continued)

(Continued)

Three ICWs

Using the same sort of objects, the adult increases the information carrying word complexity by adding in prepositions or by adding meaning.

- 'Brush teddy's foot.'
- 'Wash dolly's hand.'
- 'Put the brush under dolly.'
- 'Give me' (with your hand out) 'the cup, spoon and car.'

- I can give a simple instruction (with the same ICW breakdown) (C3.14).
- I can collect a labelled item when sent on a task (with different supports).
- I can deliver a message (with different supports).
- I can initiate a greeting:

  o to a familiar person (in different situations);
  o to an unfamiliar person (in different situations).

- I can take turns in a group:

  o I can take turns in a one-to-one situation with an adult.
  o I can wait for my turn in an adult-led game.
  o I can anticipate my turn in a game.

- I can lead a familiar activity:

  o circle;
  o snack;
  o a game.

All these skills are based on activities that can be carried out in a classroom; they are all working on the pre-skills of listening and talking.

Writing (C5)

In order to write, a child has to have a reasonable level of hand–eye co-ordination, so the planning of early experiences working towards the skills of writing involves planning for using hands in a variety of tasks. Writing starts with the basics of using hands functionally and breaks this down into the very early functional use:

- I can use my hands functionally.

  o I can instinctively grasp an object when it is placed in my hand.

Some readers may feel that these skills start at too low a level. However, we have had experience of several children in our school who, when you hand objects to them, just let the objects fall out of their hands.

  o I can reach out and grasp using a whole hand.
  o I can explore objects before releasing.
  o I can grasp and release an object voluntarily, etc. (C5.1).

- I can co-ordinate the use of my hands and eyes.

  - I can use stacking toys.
  - I can use a peg board.
  - I can screw and unscrew lids.
  - I can build with blocks.
  - I can build with duplo toys, etc. (C5.2).

Figure 4.9a   Using hands in a variety of tasks to learn to write

Figure 4.9b   Using hands in a variety of tasks to learn to write

These are the types of activities engaged in a box work:

- I can use a writing implement.

  - I can use a spreading action.
  - I can hold a writing implement.
  - I can make marks with a writing implement.
  - I can cover a large sheet of paper with a crayon, etc. (C5.3).

Many experiences include drawing circles and faces, and joining dot to dots.

- I can write letters.
  - I can trace lower case letters, etc.

However, writing also involves communication of ideas and writing stories without necessarily using writing:

- I can build a short story:
  - using photos;
  - using symbols;
  - using speech;
  - using text;
  - using computer programs (C10.15).

Story books (C8 and C10)

Many children with SCLD enjoy stories. They have particular favourites and they generally love repetition of familiar stories. Stories are an important part of the curriculum at our school and are carefully developed to enable the children to understand them. Puppets, dressing-up clothes, acting out the stories, rewrites of stories in simpler language with symbol support are all part of the scaffolding we offer children to engage in literature and can be planned for using *Learning Tracks* (C8).

Case Study

I'm going on a bear hunt (Rosen, 1989)

The story had been read many times in the Literacy Group and was a favourite story. The young people had sequenced the order of the story using cards and added appropriate tag lines – often repeated phrases from the story – 'We're not scared'. The class then took a bear to Flotterstone in the Pentland Hills near Edinburgh, a favourite outside place used by the school. Here they found 'long wavy grass' and took themselves through it, 'thick oozy mud' and likewise took themselves through it, gradually building up the story and eventually finding the bear in a cave. The experience was repeated and eventually filmed and shared with the rest of the school in assembly.

Information books and posters

Just like any other school, we do projects and themes covering the full breadth of the curriculum. We encourage commenting, questioning, answering questions, identifying, labelling, sorting, matching – all of which are included in *Learning Tracks* (M13).

Conclusion

The vast majority of our pupils enter school with very few communication skills. The greatest proportion of our teaching time is spent on helping our pupils to learn to communicate. The vast majority leave our school with some communication skills, usually using symbols or some speech supported by symbols. A few pupils still have very little understanding or use of any formal communication when they leave school. This is because of wide-scale damage to their declarative memory (Boucher et al., 2008). *Learning Tracks* is a booklet that the young people take with them when they leave school; it gives a clear record of learning for people who will work with them post-school, down to the level of words and signs that they know (or have known).

References

American Psychiatric Association (ed.) (2000) *DSM-IV Diagnostic and Statistical Manual of Mental Disorders*. Washington, DC: American Psychiatric Association.

Attwood, A.J. (1998) *Asperger's Syndrome: A Guide for Parents and Professionals*. London: Jessica Kingsley.

Bondy, A. and Frost, L. (2001) The Picture Exchange Communication System. *Behaviour Modification*, 25(5): 725–44.

Boucher, J., Mayes, A. and Bigham, S. (2008) Memory, language and intellectual ability in low-functioning autism. In Boucher, J. and Bowler, D. (eds) *Memory in Autism*. New York: Cambridge University Press.

Caldwell, P. (2006) *Finding You Finding Me*. London: Jessica Kingsley.

Carpenter, M., Nagell, K. and Thomasello, M. (1998) Social cognition, joint attention and communicative competence from 9–15 months of age. *Monographs of the Society for Research in Child Development*, 63(4): 1–163.

Charman, T., Drew, A., Baird, C. and Baird, G. (2003) Measuring early language development in pre-school children with an ASD spectrum disorder using the Macarther Communicative Development Inventory (infant form). *Journal of Child Language*, 30: 213–36.

Donnelley, R.R. (2008) Curriculum for Excellence. Building the curriculum 3: A framework for learning and teaching (p. 8) (www.educationscotland.gov.uk/images/building_the_curriculum_3_jms3_tcm4-489454.pdf, accessed 5 October 2015).

Goldstein, H. (2002) Communication intervention for children with autism: A review of treatment efficacy. *Journal of Autism and Developmental Disorders*, 32(5): 373–96.

Hind, M. (1999) Intensive interaction and autism: A useful approach. *British Journal of Special Education*, 26(2): 96–102.

Intensive Interaction (www.intensiveinteraction.co.uk, accessed 5 October 2015).

Knowles, W. and Masidlover, M. (1982) The Derbyshire Language Scheme. Published by Derbyshire County Council.

Koegel, R.L. and Johnson, J. (1989) Motivating language use in autistic children. In Dawson, G. (ed.) *Autism: Nature Diagnosis and Treatment*. New York: Guildford.

Lindsley, O. (1964) Direct measurement and prosthesis of retarded behaviour. *Journal of Education*, 147: 62–81.

Marwick, H.M., Jarvie, K., Johnston, L., Cowie, H., Quinn, N. and Cunningham, R. (2013) 'Developing symbolic play for children with autism using a joint-play intervention'. In European Early Childhood Educational Research Association Conference (EECERA), Tallin, 28 August 2013.

Rosen, M. (1989) *We're Going on a Bear Hunt*. London: Walker.

Rutherford, M.D., Young, G.S., Hepburn, S. and Rogers, S.J. (2007) A longtitudinal study of pretend play in autism: A comparative study. *Journal of Autism and Developmental Disorders,* 37(6): 1024–39.

Statutory Guidance, National Curriculum in England: English programmes of study (July 2014) (www.gov.uk/government/publications/national-curriculum-in-england-english-programmes-of-study/national-curriculum-in-england-english-programmes-of-study, accessed 5 October 2015).

Williams, J. (2008) Self–other relations in social development and autism: Multiple roles for mirror neurons and other brain bases. *Autism Research*, 1: 73–90.

5

Health and Wellbeing

Maslow's hierarchy of needs

Abraham Maslow (1909–1970) in his 1943 paper 'A theory of human motivation' refuted behaviourism because it was based on animal research and instead posited a motivational model for human behaviour known as 'Maslow's hierarchy of needs'.

His theory proposes that 'man is a perpetually wanting animal' (Maslow, 1943: 370), and his needs are arranged in a hierarchy of pre-potency – i.e. the first set of needs are more powerful than the second set of needs and would gain priority of action.

1. The first and most powerful needs are physiological needs:

    Air, food, drink, shelter, warmth, sex, sleep.

These include homeostasis, which is the body's automatic efforts to maintain a normal state of the bloodstream (sufficient water, salt, protein, fat, calcium, oxygen content, etc.). If the body feels that it is lacking some component, the person will tend to develop a particular appetite for a food containing that element. Other physiological needs are: sleep, thirst, sexual desire and maternal behaviour.

Maslow considered that physiological needs were the most pre-potent; that a person lacking food, safety, love and esteem would usually hunger for food more than anything else. If a person was starving, all his/her energies would be channelled towards hunger satisfaction and all s/he would be able to think about would be food.

Once physiological needs are satisfied – or mainly satisfied – the person is able to think about:

2. Safety needs:

    Security, order, stability, freedom from fear, health.

Maslow considered that in the same way that a physiological need can dominate all thought and action, so can a safety need. He used young children's behaviour in his explanations because he perceived adults as having learnt to hide their reactions to fear. Very young children react as if they were in danger when they are disturbed, or dropped, or experience loud noises. According to Maslow, illness makes a child feel unsafe and pain or vomiting can create fear: 'at moments of pain the whole world changes from sunniness to darkness and becomes a place where anything might happen' (Maslow, 1943: 377).

Stability disappears

Maslow stresses the importance of stability for the child, undisrupted routines and a predictable, orderly life. Inconsistency makes the child feel anxious and unsafe. Presenting a child with unfamiliar or strange stimuli or situations can elicit a danger or terror reaction, often clinging to a parent or carer in their role of protector.

For the adult population in our generally safe society, the resources for managing safety are only mobilised in times of emergency such as war, disease, catastrophe and accidents. This is, with a major exception of the neurotic adult, for example, obsessive compulsives who try to order their world so that no unfamiliar and unexpected changes will appear.

Once safety needs are sufficiently satisfied:

3. Love needs:

Friendship, intimacy, affection, love from family, friends and partners.

The person will then 'hunger' for affection and belonging to a social group. Thwarting these needs leads to maladjustment and psychotherapy:

4. Self-esteem.

Achievement, independence, status, respect and self-respect.

Humans need:

a. Confidence and respect.
b. Independence and freedom.

Satisfaction of self-esteem needs leads to self-confidence, worth, capability and a feeling of being useful, which is the basis of emotional literacy. Thwarting this need leads to feelings of worthlessness and helplessness.

Once all these needs have been sufficiently satisfied:

c. Self-actualisation:

The striving for achievement of personal potential and self-fulfilment – the truly satisfied and contented person.

Maslow later added three additional needs: two after self-esteem – cognitive needs and aesthetic needs; and one after self-actualisation – self-transcendence needs (spiritual needs).

Maslow's ideas have implications for schools. It implies that hungry or tired children will not be able to engage in learning; they will be focusing on their need for food or sleep. Sensory processing difficulties fit into the first level of physiological needs, which implies that children distressed or focusing on sensory input such as noise will be unable to engage in learning. This is most easily seen with noise; children with their fingers in their ears making lots of blocking-out noise themselves cannot respond to any teaching sounds and cannot use their hands to do anything educational. So it is important to design classrooms to minimise sensory difficulties.

Children who are unwell will not be able to engage in learning. Children who feel unsafe will also find it difficult to engage in learning; their need for safety will preoccupy them. This is particularly pertinent for children with SCLD and children with an ASD who demonstrably feel unsafe in school, and makes it incumbent on the teachers to maximise their pupils' feelings of security.

The health and wellbeing of many children with SCLD in school is very dependent on the way they are treated. It is impossible to discuss this part of the curriculum without considering the role of teachers and class teams, so it is a significant component of this chapter.

The Curriculum Area of Health and Wellbeing

Health and wellbeing includes:

- Health.
- Emotional literacy:

  o social relationships and understanding of others;
  o understanding and management of self.

- Self-care.
- Safety.
- Physical activity.
- Relationships, sexual health and parenthood.
- Other life skills.

Health and wellbeing is the absolute kingpin of the classroom for children with SCLD. There are nearly always health issues; it seems that a damaged/different brain affects body functions. The teacher needs to be familiar with what every individual's issues are and how these issues affect the pupils' wellbeing and learning. They need to observe closely changes in behaviour that might indicate that something is wrong, as the child is very unlikely to be able to communicate what is wrong except by behaviour, which is a blunt tool for the task, often impossible to interpret.

Health

Common health issues include:

1. Sleep problems.

Sleep is a significant problem for 40–80 per cent of children with ASD (Eggerding, 2010). Bartlett et al. (1985) studied sleeping difficulties of children with learning difficulties and reported a prevalence of sleeping problems of:

- 86 per cent under 6 years;
- 81 per cent from 6 to 11 years;
- 77 per cent from 12 to 16 years.

In our school most children suffer from sleeping problems. These problems include getting to sleep, staying asleep, getting back to sleep after waking and sleep apnoea.

Studies suggest that children with an ASD are more likely to have circadian rhythm (natural wake/sleep cycles) disturbances and abnormal melatonin regulation. Melatonin is the hormone that regulates the sleep/wake cycles. Many pupils at our school take melatonin in an attempt to regulate their sleeping (prescribed by the hospital) with varying degrees of success. One of the problems of taking melatonin is that there must be breaks when it is not taken. Other medical problems such as bowel problems or mental health problems can also disrupt sleep. Drugs taken to support behavioural issues can interfere with sleep. Insufficient sleep impacts on daytime behaviour, making challenging behaviour more challenging; it also impacts on the children's learning, and on all areas of health and wellbeing. It is also a massive problem for families.

2. Gastrointestinal problems.

Very many children with SCLD and/or ASD suffer from gastrointestinal problems. The main evidences of this are constipation, diarrhoea and vomiting. All these conditions are accompanied by pain and discomfort, and are usually chronic. Valicent-McDermott et al. (2006) undertook a study comparing the prevalence of gastrointestinal symptoms in children with an ASD, children with typical development and children with other developmental disabilities. The results were:

- Children with ASD: 70 per cent.
- Children with other developmental disabilities: 42 per cent.
- Typically developing children: 28 per cent.

Coury et al. (2012), when planning a research agenda on this very problem, stated that the underlying nature of this gastrointestinal dysfunction is poorly understood (hence the need for research) but that it may be due to immune dysfunction, problems with signalling pathways between the gut and brain, changes in gut flora or inflammation of the intestinal tract.

Gastrointestinal problems impinge greatly on toilet-training, behaviour and wellbeing. Children can fear going to the toilet, as going to the toilet when constipated can be painful and therefore they fear going; others may have issues with the 'coming away' of the bowel movement and will attempt to control their bowels in a manner which usually makes things worse. Some children with these problems are in pain and discomfort most of the time. Five out of six of our case study children have gastro-intestinal problems.

3. Epilepsy.

In Part 1, we reported that the prevalence rate for epilepsy among people with learning disabilities is at least 20 times higher than the general population. Epilepsy can make a person feel really bad, both before, but more so after a seizure; most people need to sleep to recover. Some children have epileptic activity nearly every day. Such children are unwell most of the time. Blair (case study, pp. 17–18) has epilepsy, which impinges greatly on his behaviour.

4. Sensory issues.

Many children with an ASD have difficulty processing everyday sensory information such as sounds, sights and smells. This can be called 'sensory integration difficulties', or 'sensory sensitivity'. It can have a profound effect on a person's life. There are seven senses and people with an ASD can be oversensitive (hyper) or under-sensitive (hypo) to any of these senses. Sensory issues are also evident in children with SCLD without a diagnosis of an ASD.

Table 5.1 Sensitivities table

Sense	Hyposensitive (under)	Hypersensitive (over)
Sight	Objects may appear dark, central vision blurry, poor depth perception – problems with throwing and catching.	May have distorted vision, images may fragment, bright lights hurt, may focus on detail rather than on the whole. May flicker hands in front of face.
Sound	May hear sounds in only one ear, may not hear some sounds, might love loud noisy places and making lots of noise.	Noises may be muddle, distorted and painful. May not be able to cut out background sounds. Very sensitive to sound. Might put fingers in ears and make lots of noise to cut out other noise.
Touch	High pain threshold may self-harm'; likes deep pressure and holds things very tightly.	Touch can be painful, might not like to be touched. Might not like clothes, particularly shoes and gloves. Difficulties with washing and brushing hair. May only like certain types of clothing/textures.
Taste	Likes spicy food – might eat anything playdough/grass (pica).	Some flavours and foods too strong and some textures uncomfortable – may have a restricted diet – only eats smooth white foods.
Smell	No sense of smell – may lick things for information.	Smells can be overwhelming – can cause toileting problems. Dislike of people's smells (perfumes, etc.).
Balance vestibular	Need to rock, swing or spin to get sensory input.	Difficulties with activities where need to control movements. Motion sickness.
Body awareness (proprioception)	Stands too close to people – cannot measure proximity, bumps into people and things.	Difficulties with fine motor skills – moves the whole body to look at something.

Source: The National Autistic Society

Sensory issues impinge greatly on behaviour, learning and wellbeing. Sometimes, hypersensitivity causes sensory overload and this sensory overload is so high that it engages the **fight, flight or freeze** mechanism, children run away or lash out, or **drop** and refuse to move. Children with SCLD cannot tell people what is wrong; teachers have to observe their behaviour to assess what is causing distress. Next, the teacher should respond by, if possible, removing or mitigating the cause of the distress. Preferred environments for teaching children with SCLD and/or an ASD should have natural light (definitely not fluorescent lighting) and blinds (cuts out over-bright sunshine), an uncluttered calm appearance, including reasonably bare walls, floor coverings and wall coverings that minimise sounds (scraping of chairs and echoing), plenty of space, preferably with additional quiet rooms and enclosed workstations, an isolated place with their own favourite things, and a door to an outside area with green space. Five out of six of our case study children have sensory issues.

Proprioceptive issues can be helped by using **weighted waistcoats** or other weighted objects (scarves, blankets, lap pillows) to give children and young people appropriate calming sensory feedback. Being tightly wrapped in a blanket or wearing a compression vest can help as well (case study, Blair, pp. 17–18).

5. Undiagnosed medical problems.

It is difficult to diagnose medical problems in children with SCLD. Their presentation of pain is atypical and their communication skills forestall discussion. Medical professionals generally do not have a lot of training in how to communicate with children with SCLD and even their parents frequently do not know what is wrong. One area Lindy has always been concerned with is migraines. She has never had a child diagnosed with migraine, but by observation has felt that quite a few of her class have suffered from them from time to time, but this is so difficult to diagnose that there is no medication to alleviate the symptoms. This is true of much pain that children with SCLD experience.

Tracking children's learning in health

In *Learning Tracks* we particularly focus on:

- Using exercise to keep healthy (H18–22).
- Eating a balanced diet (H23–26).
- Keeping clean, including toileting (H27).
- Knowing about and asking for medicine (H29).
- Looking after his/her body, including privacy, etc. (H34–37).
- Learning about living things and looking after a baby (H38–39).

Emotional Literacy

A large part of the Health and Wellbeing area of the Curriculum for Excellence is concerned with the concepts of Emotional Intelligence/Literacy. Since the 1990s, researchers have been interested in the role of emotions in all aspects of life. Daniel Goleman (1996) considers that Emotional Intelligence is more significant than IQ in predicting successful lives.

Emotional Intelligence includes the ability to:

- Understand other people's feelings.
- Have empathy for others.
- Establish and maintain relationships.
- Identify and understand one's own feelings.
- Manage one's own feelings constructively.
- Regulate one's own behaviour.

Compare this list to the list of an ASD's core deficits:

1. Social communication.

Cannot communicate their needs and feelings.
   Do not understand other people's attempts to communicate with them.

2. Social interaction.

Do not engage in joint attention, are not motivated to share information and experiences.
   Do not understand Theory of Mind – that is, don't understand that other people have different points of view and don't understand that others don't necessarily know what they know.
   Find other people frightening, confusing and unpredictable.

3. Imagination, thought and behaviour.

Do not engage in imaginative or social play.
   Lack imitation skills.
   Due to episodic memory problems – cannot remember things that have happened to them.
   Have little understanding of self.
   Rigidity of thought and behaviour.
   Table 5.2 compares these side by side.

Table 5.2   Emotional Intelligence skills table

Emotional Intelligence skills	ASD difficulties
Identify and understand one's own feelings	Have little understanding of self.
	Cannot communicate their needs and feelings.
	Due to episodic memory problems, cannot remember things that have happened to them.
Manage one's own feelings constructively	Have little understanding of self.
	Due to episodic memory problems, cannot remember things that have happened to them.
Regulate one's own behaviour	Have little understanding of self.
Understand other people's feelings	Do not understand Theory of Mind – i.e. don't understand that other people have different points of view and don't understand that others don't necessarily know what they know.
	Do not understand other people's attempts to communicate with them.
	Do not engage in joint attention – are not motivated to share information and experiences.
	Find other people frightening and confusing.
Have empathy for others	Do not understand Theory of Mind – i.e. don't understand that other people have different points of view and don't understand that others don't necessarily know what they know.
Establish and maintain relationships	Do not understand other people's attempts to communicate with them.
	Do not engage in joint attention – are not motivated to share information and experiences.
	Find other people frightening and confusing.
	Do not engage in imaginative or social play (relationships in childhood are mainly developed through play).

Then consider developmental age; most children with SCLD are at an experiential or contextual phase.
   Children functioning at an experiential phase would generally do the following:
   Play cooperatively with an adult, play alongside others, demonstrate a sense of self and want to be independent, say no to an adult, be aware of others' feelings – i.e. look concerned about crying (DfE, 2013).

Children functioning at a contextual phase would generally do the following:

Be interested in others' play and start to join in. Express their own feelings such as being sad, happy, scared, cross and worried, express their own preferences and interests, seek out others to share experiences, inhibit their own actions/behaviours – e.g. stop themselves from doing something they shouldn't do, show some understanding and cooperate with some boundaries and routines, respond to the feelings and wishes of others (DfE, 2013).

However, in our experience, children with SCLD even without a diagnosis of ASD struggle with these very early skills. This is a core area of difficulty for people with an ASD, so they need a lot of help and support to understand even apparently simple concepts such as like and dislike. This learning starts with interaction, so learning in this area can be planned for and tracked in Communication and Literacy as well as in Health and Wellbeing.

Tracking children's learning in Emotional Intelligence/Literacy

Emotional literacy learning divides into two broad elements:

1. Social relationship and understanding of others (being with others):

   a. playing with others;
   b. paying attention to others.

2. Understanding and management of self:

   a. recognising own simple emotions;
   b. learning useful responses to emotions.

Table 5.3 looks specifically at our case study children.

Table 5.3   Emotional Literacy and case study children

	Being with others	Playing with others	Paying attention to others	Recognises own simple emotions	Has learnt useful responses to own emotions
Andrew	Only with support, usually to do with food	Only adults	No	No	No
Ewan	In structured situations when calm	Only adults	Only to be wary except in supported structured situations	Like/dislike Can say yes and no	Yes – learning
Isla	Only with support	Only adults	Interested but often in a negative way	No	No
Donald	Only with support	Only adults	Scared of people but loves watching them	Like /dislike for concrete things Yes/no	When supported, can make appropriate choices
Dougal	In structured situations	Only adults or other children in extremely structured adult-led situations	Not independently – in supported structured situations	Like/dislike Happy and sad	No
Blair	In structured situations when calm with support	Only adults or other children in extremely structured adult-led situations	Not independently except to be wary – in supported structured situations Likes to people-watch	Like/dislike Can name emotions on photo cards, learnt by rote, but with little or no understanding	Yes, but learning breaks down under stress

Social relationships and understanding of others

1. Being with others (C3, C10, H6, H8, H33).

This is an area in which we invest an enormous amount of time and energy. Children with SCLD/ASD find others frightening and simply don't want to be with them. However, the alternative to a social life is isolation. Despite finding relationships immensely difficult, most people with an ASD do not actually want to be isolated (Muller et al., 2008) and much research on isolation and loneliness concludes that they are profoundly negative experiences for human beings and affect both health and wellbeing (Jaremka et al., 2013). So, allowing our children to isolate themselves is not an option.

Hence from the beginning of school we plan for socialisation. Actually, throughout the school a very large proportion of our pupils' learning experiences are to do with socialisation. This is tracked in C3 and C10, H6 and H8.

Many of our lessons are about being with others. In one class Lindy taught, they baked a chocolate cake every week for a year. The learning was not about baking; the baking was the motivation. Everybody, at some level or another, understood that the end result was chocolate cake, to be eaten as soon as it was baked. The learning was about sitting on a chair appropriately, joint attention, waiting for and taking a turn, passing an object to another pupil; the learning was about being with others.

Nearly all group-work lessons are about the group first and the lesson second. Many group-work activities are chosen for the motivation; another good example is sensory play – cornflour gloop, dried lentils, baked beans or spaghetti (many of our sensory play material are edible because much of it ends up in mouths).

Many of our group-work lessons are very repetitive because our pupils need to recognise what is going to happen in order to be relaxed enough to engage in the activity. In the primary classes, a lesson usually starts with a song which is signed and supported with the appropriate symbol.

'Is everybody ready? It's time for circle. Is everybody ready? It's time for circle.'

There is also a song at the end.

'Circle's finished. Circle's finished. Time to stop. Time to stop. Circle's finished. Circle's finished. Time to stop … or time for whatever comes next – snack?'

Songs can be very helpful in building up the routine and familiarity necessary in a classroom for children with SCLD.

Once a week there is assembly, with very nearly the whole school; this is not a quiet, contemplative occasion; it can be quite noisy and chaotic. The learning is about being with more people. Pupils come and go, and participate from the corridor.

2. Playing with others (C10).

Most children in our school only interact with or pay attention to adults, and the adults take the lead; this is actually appropriate for their developmental ages. Some of our more able children can engage in structured play – e.g. bingo, pairs or lotto, or rehearsed drama situations such as 'I am going on a bear hunt' (Rosen, 1989), described in Part 2. We find that pupils engage better in social activities at Forest School than they do at school – for example, playing follow-my-leader (supported by holding a rope) and hide-and-seek. We think that this is because they find the setting calming.

3. Paying attention to others (C3).

Not every child in our school has a diagnosis on the autistic spectrum and this is an area where the differences between the children with an ASD and without an ASD are most evident. For instance, John even as a very young boy (5–6 years of age) would notice when one of his peers was upset. Without prompting, he would fetch whatever it was that that particular child liked best and give it to the child. He had empathy, he knew that upset children needed comforting and he also knew his peers well enough to know what would comfort each individual child. The children without an ASD can be significantly more interested and knowledgeable about their peers. The children with ASD need support to pay attention to their peers. Structured situations offer opportunities for supporting attention to others – for example, responding to greetings in circle, and taking turns and leading simple table-top and circle games (C3).

Understanding and management of self

4. Recognising own simple emotions (H1–3, H5).

Here we start with like and dislike. This is surprisingly difficult. First, we label like and dislike for the children. Children are encouraged to review their learning experiences, to communicate whether they liked or disliked it initially by tapping the like or dislike symbol. Many children still require support to do this at 18 years of age.

Labelling like and dislike and emotions is incredibly challenging as the adult has to be absolutely sure that the child has experienced that feeling in order to correctly label it and support the child to recognise it in the future. Sometimes a negative reaction isn't in relation to the activity, but perhaps the noise going on around them or perhaps they are hungry, so knowing the children well and what their responses look like is incredibly important before labelling begins.

Next comes happy and sad; again, we label the children's emotions for them (which is not always easy) and then encourage them to communicate whether they are happy or sad. Very few children get beyond that, but the opportunity to track simple emotions can be found in H1.

Case Study

Labelling emotions

Blair has had many incidents of challenging behaviour and is able enough to review these incidents later. Adults labelled his emotion to him as 'a little bit upset', when actually what they meant was that he was wildly, wildly distressed. Unfortunately, he has learnt the label and now uses it when he is wildly distressed. This is not a problem in school as we can translate, but not useful in the wider world. We are working on a range of vocabulary to help him describe how he feels, starting with 'a little bit worried', genuinely at the start of the problem so that calming strategies can be brought in early before a meltdown.

5. Learning useful responses to emotions.

One particular area of great difficulty that impinges on everything else is behaving in a socially acceptable way, and this is due to a lack of social understanding and an inability to communicate their feelings and needs in any other way than by behaviour, and it is this behaviour that is often unacceptable. Everybody is familiar with the 'terrible twos tantrums', evident in any supermarket from time to time; with a person with SCLD, you have an 'overgrown 2-year-old' with strong desires and needs but with, generally, less communication skills and social understanding than a 2-year-old. The result can be, and often is, violent behaviour such as biting, extreme hair-pulling, scratching, hitting, kicking and punching.

Challenging behaviour

'Challenging behaviour' is an interesting term; first, what is challenging to one person may not be challenging to another. The use of the term 'challenging behaviour' to describe severely problematic and socially unacceptable behaviour was chosen to focus teachers and carers on responding to the behaviour as a challenge to their skills. Services like schools need to design positive behaviour plans to reduce the behaviour to allow the children to continue to access education (Felce and Emerson, 1966). Most schools have a positive behaviour policy.

Challenging behaviour can be defined as behaviour that is likely to injure someone badly (including the perpetrator) or destroy part of their environment, or behaviour that is likely to limit access to the use of ordinary community facilities – in this case, school (Emerson et al., 1988). Usually, the definition also includes some aspect of frequency such as daily, and often includes reference to the need for the physical intervention of more than one member of staff.

Challenging behaviour is linked to intellectual disability – the more severe the disability, the more likelihood of challenging behaviour (Jang et al., 2011). This is easily explained by the fact that the more disabled a person is, the less access they have to resources such as language to communicate their desires and needs or understand information.

Challenging behaviour is linked to autistic spectrum disorders. One study concluded that 94.3 per cent of children and adolescents display at least one challenging behaviour (Matson et al., 2010).

Comorbidity of intellectual disability and ASD increases the risk of challenging behaviour (O'Brien and Pearson, 2004). So, a child with SCLD is highly likely to display challenging behaviour, and a child with SCLD and ASD will almost definitely display challenging behaviour. In our school, all the children display behaviours that some people find challenging, though not all at the level described above. Most of our pupils by adolescence have at least a dual diagnosis (ASD and SCLD – see Case Studies).

Normalisation has been the largest movement in social and educational policy in the past 40 years. However, more recently inclusion, particularly inclusive education, has been an increasingly dominant philosophy. While normalisation and inclusion are different in direction, they have the same aim – for people with a learning disability to be valued in society. Normalisation has done a lot to move away from institutionalisation and towards community-based services. However, the next steps now need to be taken. Much of the move away from normalisation has stemmed from the belief that normalisation means that those individuals with a learning disability need to change and 'normalise' their difference, and for them to conform in order to be accepted. Both Nirje and Wolfsenberger (cited in Culham and Nind, 2003), by adopting the term 'social role valorisation' (SRV), have tried to redefine normalisation to be about being valued in 'normal' society. However, inclusion goes one step further. Normalisation and SRV have both focused to some level on the denial of difference and have valued conformity, while for inclusion, difference is ordinary. Inclusion is different from integration as it is the school/service that has to adapt to meet the needs of the individuals, not the individuals conforming to be accepted. Inclusion is not conditional; it is a human right. Inclusion has to be the basis for all education policy and the main value base.

Challenging behaviour can come from two routes:

- A person will lash out or use some other physical communication because they do not have access to other means of communication to inform that they need/want something or really do not want to do something or be in a particular place – fight or flight.
- A person has learnt over time that if they present with this behaviour they will be removed from the experience/place which they don't want to do or where they don't want to be.

Challenging behaviour is not always violent; there are many challenging behaviours that result in a child being unable to access ordinary facilities such as:

- Various levels of refusing, including dropping to the floor and refusing to move, which can cause particular difficulties in the community – for instance, when crossing the road.
- Stripping off clothes, which is also difficult in public.
- Self-harm in its extreme form is probably the behaviour that staff find hardest to deal with.
- Repetitive or stereotypical behaviour (prevents engagement in other activities).

Repetitive or stereotypical behaviour

This covers a wide range of behaviours:

- repeatedly flicking their fingers or an object such as a piece of string;
- lining things up;
- lengthy rituals;
- odd body movements;
- insistence on following identical routes.

Nearly all our pupils demonstrate stereotypical behaviours – see the chapter on Case Studies for stereotypical behaviour (special interests). Andrew derives great pleasure from holding a handful of lentils high above his head and sprinkling them down into a bowl. He would happily spend all day doing this.

These behaviours can be all-consuming of the children's interests. When engaged in the behaviours, the children can be very difficult to reach or to engage in anything else. The function of the behaviours tends to vary – for example:

- Play: this is the way our children play, how they choose to spend their time, what they enjoy doing; it is not wrong and we should respect their right to play like this.
- Escape: children will choose to engage in these activities when life becomes too stressful; this is a good strategy and should be recognised and encouraged – that is, the child should be helped to recognise when stress levels are getting too high and ask for their preferred object (I call them comforters, because that is what they are). These activities are tracked as calming techniques (H4).
- Blocking: children choose to engage in the activity prior to anything becoming stressful, to block out any other activity and this is a use that teachers often find challenging. It is counter-productive simply to take away the comforters or refuse to allow them in the classroom. These comforters make great rewards. They are really motivating. At the same time they can get in the way of planned teaching activities, but encouraging a child to put their obsessional objects/behaviour away and engage in another planned activity needs to be sensitively and systematically handled; learning to do this will be the learning experience. It helps when engaging the child in this learning if the other activity is a preferred activity.
- Routines that children have got themselves into and cannot let go of, for example touching particular objects on a journey.

Challenging behaviour is always purposeful and meaningful, but it is sometimes a challenge for teachers to work out, and that is where functional analysis comes in.

When a child engages in challenging behaviour, a class team have initially to manage it in such a way as to limit damage. The next step is to establish the function of the behaviour and the most common analysis is ABC – Antecedent, Behaviour, Consequence (Functional Analysis derived from Applied Behavioural Analysis, ABA).

- Antecedent.

What happened before the behaviour: this may consist of a very recent event such as someone spilt his juice, or involve a build-up of events which caused the young person to become distressed – for example:

1. The taxi that brought him to school was late.
2. The person who usually escorted him to class did not meet him.
3. Someone had put their coat on his hook.
4. He was late for circle, and so on.

- Behaviour.

What was the behaviour?

- Consequence.

What happened as a result of the behaviour?

Did s/he get what s/he wanted?

- Next functional analysis.

What was the function of the behaviour?

Usually one of:

- Escape – to leave the situation.
- To get something.
- To get attention: a person never seeks attention they don't need, so this is not a negative – they just need to be taught better ways of getting the attention they need.

Once a theory is established, a plan can be made to attempt to eliminate the behaviour. Unfortunately, often the challenging behaviour is very complex and it is really difficult to establish its function. Here, a tentative theory has to be worked on to enable trialling of different actions which could help to clarify the situation.

Antecedent analysis

Sometimes, the behaviour can be completely avoided by eliminating the antecedent. This is something that the class team can actually have power over:

a. It could be 'something' wrong in the environment – too much noise, a dislike of sitting near a particular person – which could be changed.
b. The activity is new or they had a bad experience last time, so they believe that is what the activity is. They need to encounter the experience positively and build on this slowly with gradual increases that they can be supported to cope with it.
c. It could be an unreal expectation such as expecting a child to sit in circle for half an hour when he just can't do it. Strangely enough, teachers/class teams are often reluctant to change some of these environmental factors even though a child might scratch and bite for 20 minutes in circle every day, they can still be unwilling to use the staggered circle strategy where different pupils stay for different lengths of time. Comments are made like 'Everybody has to stay for circle.'

This is a very serious point of concern that teachers/class teams need to address and it generally stems from:

a. The staff's lack of understanding of the children's difficulties, either diagnosis or developmental level. Support staff are generally untrained and some teachers have little experience in this area, and with little in-service time during the year, it takes a long time to develop a true understanding of the children's difficulties.
b. When staff are working with challenging children, they themselves are under stress and, just as stress causes children with an ASD and/or SCLD to behave rigidly and inflexibly, so too it causes staff to behave rigidly and inflexibly just when they need to be super-flexible with these rigid, inflexible children (autistic behaviour is, after all, just an extreme form of normal human behaviour).
c. Staff need to understand anxiety and how to support children through this; give them short, successful experiences and slowly build on these.

So, teachers/class teams have to make a considerable effort to analyse situations and truthfully evaluate whether there is something they can do differently to make the situation better. Sometimes a critical friend can help do this – as long as it is a sensitive critical friend.

Next, a plan has to be drawn up based on this analysis.

A proactive plan

A proactive plan describes what to do on a day-to-day basis to help minimise the likelihood of the challenging behaviour, these might be:

- Looking for triggers and either removing or minimalising them (antecedent control strategies).
- Changing the environment.
- Stepping back the level of demand, particularly at times of stress.
- Setting up a reward system.
- Teaching replacement skills (functional equivalents) such as using symbols to ask for something or escape.
- Teaching the use of, for example, a weighted waistcoat to help with proprioceptive sensory problems.
- Organising routine and structure to create a feeling of safety.
- Teaching new skills leading to coping and tolerance.
- Focused support strategies to achieve control over behaviour.

A reactive plan

A reactive plan describes what to do and how one should react in response to a child's challenging behaviour. These might include:

- Ignoring the behaviour (but not the child).
- Giving reminders.
- Distraction.
- Giving the person what they want.
- Withdrawal.
- As a last resort, physical intervention. Staff should be properly trained in how to use physical intervention. In our school we use **CALM (Crisis and Aggression, Limitation and Management)**.

This is a cyclic endeavour. Strategies are put in place, then observations are made and strategies are tweaked or completely changed. Sometimes, a magic key is found where one change can make a massive difference – usually, it is a patient-persistent gradual process. In this example we have used a proactive plan.

Case Study

Ewan's behaviour was punching, head-butting and kicking (sometimes to the level of hospital treatment).

The function of behaviour was to escape demands; the behaviour was reinforced because his behaviour removed him from the demands. The problem was that Ewan was so sensitive to any demands, that it seemed he could not tolerate being in any of the places we asked him to be, or doing anything we asked him to do, and this severely limited his access to education.

In addition, Ewan had terrible bowel problems and suffered a great deal of pain and discomfort. Unsurprisingly, he found demands more difficult on these days and we had to step back his demands correspondingly. He could not/would not sit on a chair on such occasions.

Strategies:

- Ewan had a good understanding of symbols. We made visual schedules for every work session so that he knew exactly what the demands were going to be.
- We varied tasks between high-demand and low-demand tasks.
- We gave Ewan more control over the tasks – choice.
- We gave him a reward at the end of each session, playing with an object that he found rewarding. TEACCH recommends using extrinsic rewards to motivate and support participation (Panerai et al., 2002).
- We gave him an escape that he could ask for when he needed it – bouncing on a physio ball – after which he would be asked if he would return to the session. The reply was usually 'yes', and if he was not ready he had extra time on the ball until he was ready. Physical escapes are usually the most effective, presumably due to the release of tension and endorphins.

Ewan's behaviour has made steady progress in a positive direction. He still needs all the above supports and particularly needs sensitive diminishment of tasks when in pain. It was sometimes difficult to stop support staff 'punishing' him by taking away his reward, and this highlights the importance in this area of everybody who works with the pupils having a thorough understanding of the issues and dealing with each child consistently.

Staff need constant training in positive behavioural support in order to implement behaviour strategies in a non-aversive way. Rae et al. (2011) found that teaching staff were largely unaware of positive programming strategies and referred to reactive strategies to deal with challenging behaviour. This study was on teachers but is true of support staff as well. It is essential that staff are consistent and have the same understandings and expectations.

CAMHS did a small study in our school regarding **adaptive skills** on the Adaptive Behaviour Assessment System II (ABAS-II). ABAS-II provides a profile that covers the adaptive skills which are life skills, consisting of:

- Conceptual skills, including reading, numbers, money, time and communication.
- Social skills, including understanding and following social rules.
- Practical life skills such as feeding, dressing and occupational skills.

The profile covers these three areas and seeks to identify priority area for intervention. The results were that the pupils of the school tested were all operating at a pre-nursery level. The staff were very surprised at the results of what the expectations of the pupils should be, compared to what they were expecting of them. It points to a need for staff to be thoroughly educated in basic child development, adaptive behaviour, communication, functional analysis of behaviour and positive behavioural support. It is also one of the reasons that a development chart is used in *Learning Tracks*. One of the greatest difficulties in the school in using *Learning Tracks* is that inexperienced staff consistently overestimate the level of ability.

When Lindy started working at the school, she set mainly academic targets and viewed challenging behaviour as something that prevented these targets from being achieved. This is back-to-front thinking. Targets that address the challenging behaviour are the most important targets enabling the young person to access education and the community. Of course, they are also generally the hardest targets. It is all part of providing the child/young person with an appropriate prosthetic environment which can support them all their life. We do not look to normalise children and young people with SCLD, but to give them supports which value their strengths and allow them to be active in their community.

The strategies in countering challenging behaviour usually involve pupils in:

- Visual schedules (M6).
- Communicating that they need to escape (H5).
- Communicating needs (C3, H2).
- Reward systems (H15).
- Calming activities (H5).

For an understanding of what they like and dislike, and triggers for challenging behaviour, see H3. See also our Case Studies for different examples of triggers and the different effective calming strategies.

Once these supporting strategies have been introduced and all is calm, it is important to remember that the reason that all is calm are the supports. Teachers should not think 'He doesn't need the support any more,' and remove the supports. If the support is removed, the behaviour will return, not necessarily straight away but definitely when any extra pressure occurs. These supports are prosthetic in the same way that a guide dog or wheelchair is prosthetic for a blind person or somebody who cannot walk.

Self-care

At 5 years old, on entry to school, children with SCLD frequently have few self-care skills. Toileting, dressing, eating a range of foods appropriately at a table and washing all require teaching. Fortunately, most of these areas of learning use the procedural memory, so although they may need careful targeting at the appropriate level for the child and a lot of practice and support, once learnt, these skills will be remembered (as long as they continue to be used/practised).

Toileting (H27)

This is a very tricky area for the following reasons:

1. Health: some children have bowel problems. It is not unusual for children to only be able to open their bowels in a warm bath at home. Enemas and other medications are routinely employed.
2. Sensory issues: some children have difficulties with toileting sensations, many children find toilet seats difficult to sit on, many hate the smells of the bathroom.
3. Fear: some children are frightened by the whole business – the feelings, things coming out of them, things going down the toilet, bathrooms, bathroom noises.
4. Awareness: some children simply do not recognise the feelings of needing the toilet.
5. Control: children can feel that they need the toilet but have no control. This is often a case of maturity, which implies that toilet-training should be attempted for a length of time and, if there is no success left for a while, allowing for development of the necessary maturity. The developmental age for toilet-training is 2–3 years of age and for independent toileting 4–6 years of age, well above the developmental age of many children and young people with SCLD. At our school, young people sometimes achieve this skill as late as 16 years of age. It is worth persevering because it makes a real difference to young people's adult opportunities.
6. Communication: even if they recognise the feelings, they may have problems communicating their need.
7. This is something that absolutely has to be worked on between school and home; it is not something that can be learnt at school and simply transferred to home. Children can be very difficult at home and families are not always able to deal with toilet-training on top of everything else.

8. It is time- and labour-intensive; a child may require frequent individual attention for considerable periods of time at not necessarily convenient times of the day.
9. It is difficult to demonstrate what you want the child to do. We write individual social stories and some computer programs can be very useful, too.

One of the six case study children will still be wearing pads when he leaves school.

Washing (H27.4)

Washing also has sensory issues but has the great advantage that it can be taught hand-over-hand, which toileting can't. Our children clean their teeth every day after lunch, which helps with general teeth hygiene as some families find it difficult to get their children to clean their teeth. Children with SCLD have notoriously bad teeth, sometimes due to using feeder bottles for much longer than normal.

Dressing (H11)

We are very lucky in our school in that we have our own swimming pool and most classes have two sessions in the pool a week, one nominally a swimming lesson and one for leisure activities. Swimming pools are great for interactions and play because the heads of the children and adults are at the same level. Going swimming also gives a reason for taking off and putting on clothing, which needs a lot of practice. If schools do not have swimming pools, scheduling in showers could be an alternative for these functional self-care opportunities.

Food (H23–26)

Children with an ASD and/or SCLD frequently have food issues:

• They won't eat food with certain textures, colour or taste.
• They will only eat, for example, white dry food such as cereals.
• They can be obsessive about food and will seek out and eat food constantly, leading to obesity, which then has its own problems.
• They put things in their mouth that isn't food such as sand or buttons. Children in general don't stop mouthing objects until around a developmental age of 5, which implies that putting things in their mouths could be expected as normal behaviour for our whole school.
• They have pica, which is a persistent and obsessive craving to eat non-food items.

Many children, when they come to school, have never sat at a table and are used to eating their food running around. Parents are more concerned, quite rightly, with actually feeding their children than with their table manners.

In school, we try to teach pupils
• To eat and enjoy a range of foods, this is important for health reasons (H24).
• To sit at a table with others (H23).
• To sit at the table and eat with reasonable table manners – this is very important because many social occasions that people with SCLD can attend and enjoy are to do with eating (H23).
• To choose food (H23).
• To eat at restaurants and cafés (H23).
• To grow food in the garden (H28).
• To go shopping for food (H25).

- To cook food; by the time they leave school, most can help prepare a simple meal (H25).
- To clear up and wash up after food (H15) (in work-related activities).
- Healthy eating (H24).

Safety

Early years outcomes (DfE, 2013) list an understanding of safety and management of some risks as developing between 40 and 60 months, which is in the generalised learning phase. Most children with SCLD do not reach this level of learning.

Children with ASD and/or SCLD tend to act impulsively and unpredictably. They are quite likely to run away or grab things with no warning. Most safety issues with these children involve adults keeping them safe. They do have some sense of danger. In seven years of teaching Forest School, Lindy experienced only one child with no fear of fire. Nevertheless, we do teach safe behaviour (usually by rote, what to do in this situation) even though they might not understand why they are doing it – for example, buckling up the seat-belt in a car.

In school, we try to teach pupils

- To stay close to their carers (H12 and H32).
- How to get help (H12 and H30).
- Road safety (H13).

People with SCLD are more vulnerable to abuse, including sexual abuse. It is very hard to teach children who have personal care needs that require pad-changing to be suspicious of people who touch them inappropriately. Likewise, as these children are cared for by a large number of people, often supply workers, how do you teach them about strangers? Some children can be taught about strangers in a contextual manner.

Case Study

Donald likes to greet people, but this can be problematic in the community. We have started working in his workbox on identifying people he knows and people who are strangers. He has learnt known phrases such as, 'I don't know.' We then began to generalise this in the community when Donald wanted to shake hands with a 'lady'. We would ask him 'Who's that?' and he would look slightly cross and sad, and say 'I don't know' and keep walking. We would then make a huge fuss of how clever he was to reinforce this and give him increased attention for this new behaviour.

We have included some experiences (H34). However, with many of the children and young people, it is the carers who have to be vigilant for the children.

Physical activity

Exercise is important for both physical and mental health. Research shows that exercise is one of the best treatments for depression. Exercise reduces stress and anxiety, and improves sleep and memory. Exercise is considered one of the most effective treatments for an ASD, decreasing stereotypical behaviour, hyperactivity, violence, self-injurious behaviour and destructiveness (Edelson, n.d.). Exercise releases endorphins, which are feel-good hormones.

Physical learning is remembered by the procedural memory, which is usually less damaged than the declarative memory, so once they have learnt a skill, children with SCLD will usually be able to remember it. Learning the skill is easy if it can be taught hand-over-hand, but it is not so easy if they have to learn with language or by imitation. Nevertheless, this is an area of the curriculum where the children are more successful.

Most young children with SCLD are lively and energetic, and enjoy physical activity. As children mature, they tend to slow down a little and sadly during the school years some become obese as they may have food obsessions.

Learning Tracks tracks the activities that our children and young people typically engage in when participating in PE and swimming lessons (H16–19). It may be that you will need to alter the content to fit your school. It also tracks other physical activity learning experiences in our school.

- Running tracks (H20).
  Every playground has a running track. All our pupils come to school by bus and taxi, and many sit for long periods of time before school. Part of some class's morning routine after toileting involves running around the running track a set number of times. This is a healthy activity and it helps fidgety pupils to sit in circle afterwards. Some of the younger classes have a small class gym session before circle.
- Playground games (H20).
  We have all sorts of playground equipment – climbing equipment, a climbing wall, scooters, roller skates, balls, trikes and go-karts – and children are encouraged to be active at playtime.
- Fitness room (H21).
  We have a room with fitness equipment with a running machine, a cycling machine, a rowing machine, a therapy ball and other exercise equipment. We teach the children to use these machines. It is part of the weakly/daily routine of nearly all pupils in the senior schools. Once they are familiar with these machines, we take them to public gyms to use the machines. This is something they can do after they leave school. For some pupils, the fitness room can be used as a place of escape from challenging (to them) activities. It has the double benefit that as well as allowing the skills to be practised, the happy hormones are released.
- Play parks (H20).
  We regularly visit play parks with our younger children. They enjoy playing in the parks, they practise turn-taking and sharing, and they engage in physical activity. Various activities can help with communication – for example, being pushed on the swing. The adult does not push until there is some form of communication asking for the push. Swinging is also a proven calming activity.
- Walks (H13 and H20).
  All classes engage in walks. The main purposes are:

  1. Going out in the community to the shops, the church, the museums, etc.
  2. Being able to walk from A to B (this can take a lot of learning; when some children start coming to school, they have never walked anywhere in public before).
  3. Learning to deal with new places and new routes.
  4. Fitness: walking is a very affordable, safe exercise that can easily be continued once they have left school.

- Cycling (H20).
  We have all sorts of bikes, including **disability bikes**. We use these bikes in the playground and we take them to safe places to cycle as well. St Crispin's engages annually in The Big Pedal.
- Forest School (H20).
  Forest School is a gentle form of outdoor education ideally suited to children with SCLD. Pupils at our school go to Forest School for half a day a week for around three years. At Forest School, they engage in physical and social activities in a calming, natural environment. Although many

pupils find it challenging at first, the majority seem to really enjoy it. One of our young people routinely fetched his cagoule and over-trousers (his Forest School kit) whenever he was feeling stressed. It was such a shame that we could not accede to his request every time he asked.

* Relationships, sexual health and parenthood.

Relationships (C3, H32, H33)

The developmental age for starting to make friends is 3 years and for friends being important is 5 years. Social interaction begins with a responsive adult. No child or young person can begin to make friends with peers without the experience and ability to socially interact with a responsive adult. Children and young people with SCLD often only play with adults (see Table 5.3).

Sexual health

It is generally agreed that children and young people with SCLD should be given sex education. The problem is how? There are learning packages available – for example, the package produced by NHS Leeds. This is a very thoughtfully produced package, but it uses language way above anything the vast majority of our young people can understand. This does not imply that one should not teach sex education, but it does imply that learners may not really understand much of it. As a result, children and young people have to be taught rules about ways to behave, such as rules for touching other people, and rules for where and when they can masturbate.

Recognition of similarities and differences (H34)

This includes 'I can sort for girls and boys.' Many young people with SCLD cannot identify gender. Developmentally, 76 per cent of 2-year-olds can identify their own gender and most 3-year-olds can identify other people's gender. Gender stability, the knowledge that girls grow up to be women and boys men, develops by 4 years of age. Gender constancy, the knowledge that gender doesn't change, develops by 7 years of age (Kohlberg, 1966).

Body awareness and respect (H34–37)

Many people with learning disabilities are sexually abused. It is fundamental that young people learn to label parts of the body, in the case of young people with SCLD this will be with appropriate symbols. They also need to sort for parts of the body that are private and can only be touched by themselves, doctors and known carers, and parts which can be touched by anyone. This is a big problem when schools and adult centres use agency staff to care for vulnerable people with intimate care needs; how can young people discriminate between people who should and shouldn't touch them?

Puberty is a difficult time for young people with SCLD. Their emotions are labile, they do not understand why and they have few ways to discuss them. Their behaviour tends to reflect their emotions. The positive aspect is that the behaviour usually calms down after puberty. Class teams have to respect their difficulties, reduce other demands on them and offer ways for them to calm down and relax. Young women need to learn about periods. Beyond Words (www.booksbeyondwords.co.uk) produces books that can help.

While people with SCLD can present with sexually inappropriate behaviour, this is driven at a hormonal level, not a cognitive level, so there is no 'understanding' behind what their body is urging them to do or how it responds.

Masturbation can be a problem. Young people need to learn where it is appropriate to masturbate. At home young people can be directed to their private place, their bedroom, but schools do not usually have such facilities. It can be difficult to teach ways of managing this behaviour, but it needs to be treated as a behaviour and redirected to a more appropriate activity in that moment, as difficult as this can be. You have to catch them at the very early stages to redirect to a motivating activity.

Caring for things and parenthood (H35, H38–39)

Learning about reproduction is included in *Learning Tracks* and caring for living things including human babies.

Other Life Skills

* Work (H15).

Once in the senior school our pupils start to learn about work. They engage in work-related activities such as housework, washing cars, cleaning the church, picking up litter (our school has its fourth Green Flag – the whole school is a star at litter-picking) and paper-shredding. Many senior pupils have regular jobs to do around the school such as delivering the milk to other classes.

Conclusion

Health and Wellbeing is the largest section of *Learning Tracks*. This is an area of the curriculum that mainly depends on the procedural memory, the memory of how to do things learnt through practice and usually relatively unimpaired in children with SCLD. This is the area of the curriculum that covers really important life skills and it is an area where our children are successful learners.

References

Bartlett, L.B., Rooney, V. and Spedding, S. (1985) Nocturnal difficulties in a population of mentally handicapped children. *British Journal of Mental Subnormality*, 31: 54–9.

Coury, D., Ashwood, P., Fasano, A., Fuch, G., Gerachty, M., Kaul, A., Maive, G., Patterson, P. and James, N. (2012) Gastrointestinal conditions in children with autistic spectrum disorder: Developing a research agenda. *Pediatrics*, 130, Supplement: 160–8.

Culham, A. and Nind, M. (2003) Deconstructing normalisation: Clearing the way for inclusion. *Journal of Intellectual and Developmental Disability*, 28(1): 65–78.

Department for Education (DfE) (2013) Early Years outcomes (www.gov.uk/government/uploads/system/uploads/attach ment_data/file/237249/Early_Years_Outcomes.pdf, accessed 5 October 2015).

Edelson, S.M. (n.d.) Physical exercise and autism (www.autism.com/treating_exercise, accessed 5 October 2015).

Eggerding, C. (2010) Put sleep difficulties to bed: Advice for parents of children with autism (www.webmd.com/brain/autism/features/sleep-difficulties-parents-autism, accessed 5 October 2015).

Emerson, E., Cummings, R., Barrett, S., Hughes, H., McCool, C. and Toogood, A. (1988) Challenging behaviour and community services: Who are the people who challenge services? *Mental Handicap*, 16: 16–19.

Felce, D. and Emerson, E. (1996) Challenging behaviour and the need for evidence-based services. *Journal of Applied Research in Intellectual Disabilities*, 91: 496–504.

Goleman, D. (1996) *Emotional Intelligence: Why it Can Matter More than IQ*. St Ives: Bloomsbury Publishing.

Jang, J., Dixon, D.R., Tarbox, J. and Granpeesheh, D. (2011) Symptom severity and challenging behaviour in children with ASD. *Research in Autism Spectrum Disorders*, 5: 1028–32.

Jaremka, L., Fagundes, C., Peng, J., Bennet, J. Glaser, R., Malarkey, W. and Kiecolt-Glaser, J. (2013) Loneliness promotes inflammation during acute stress. *Psychological Science*, 24(7): 1089–97.

Kohlberg, L. (1966) A cognitive-developmental analysis of children's sex – role concepts and attitudes. In Maccody, E.E. (ed.) *The Development of Sex Differences*. Stanford, CA: Stanford University Press.

Maslow, A. (1943) The theory of human motivation. *Psychological Review*, 50: 370–96.

Matson, J.L., Mahan, S., Hess, J. and Fodstad, D. (2010) Progression of challenging behaviors in children and adolescents with an Autism Spectrum Disorder as measured by the Autism Spectrum Disorders-Problem Behaviors for Children (ASD-PBC). *Research into An ASD Spectrum Disorders*, 4(3): 400–4.

Muller, E., Schuler, A. and Yates, G. (2008) Social challenges and supports from the perspective of individuals with Asperger Syndrome and other autistic spectrum disorders. *Autism*, 12(2): 173–90.

National Autistic Society (n.d.) The sensory world of autism (www.autism.org.uk/sensory, accessed 5 October 2015).

NHS Leeds: The Children's Disability Nursing Team (2009) Puberty and sexuality for children and young people with a learning disability (www.rsehub.org.uk/media/16503/54–Puberty-Sexuality-for-Children-and-Young-People-with-a-learning-disability.pdf, accessed 5 October 2015).

O'Brien, G. and Pearson, J. (2004) Autism and learning disability. *Autism*, 8(2): 125–40.

Panerai, S., Ferrante, L. and Zingale, M. (2002) Benefits of the TEACCH programme as compared with a non-specific approach. *Journal of Intellectual Disability Research*, 46(4): 318–27.

Rae, H., Murray, G. and McKenzie, K. (2011) Teaching staff knowledge attributions and confidence in relation to working with children with an intellectual disability and challenging behaviour. *British Journal of Learning Disabilities*, 39: 295–301.

Rosen, M. (1989) We're Going on a Bear Hunt. London: Walker.

Valicenti-McDermott, M., McVicar, K., Rapin, I., Wershil, B., Cohen, H. and Shlino, S. (2006) Frequency of gastrointestinal symptoms in children with autistic spectrum disorders and association with family history of auto-immune disease. *Journal of Developmental and Behavioural Paediatrics*, 27(2): 128–38.

Mathematics

6

Why mathematics as the third area?

Mathematics is commonly conceived as an academic subject involving abstraction, logical processing and complicated calculations, all of which seems of little relevance for the education of children with SCLD. However, mathematics is much more than that – it also consists of:

- Life skills such as sorting, matching, comparing, counting, weighing and using timetables, which are absolutely relevant to children with SCLD.
- Thinking and communicating skills, ways of thinking about things, size, shape and quantity are all part of the way we define our world. Mathematics is woven into our language and thought. Will this fit in here? We need to get the bowl first. Have we got enough juice? There will be many people at the wedding (and then what *that* implies).
- Creative skills such as pattern, rhythm and sequence (as in art, movement and music) are all a part of mathematical thinking.

By the time typically developing children start school, they will already have learnt important mathematical concepts and skills. They typically recognise numerals to five (DfE, 2013) and numerals of personal significance, can count an irregular set of objects up to ten, can order two or three more items by length, can select a named shape and can use everyday language related to time. They have been learning about mathematics since the day they were born and they learnt that mathematics through exploration and play and interaction with more knowledgeable people (parents, siblings, friends), for five years of learning.

For teachers of children with SCLD, mathematics is an interesting area of learning. In one class there can be a very wide range of ability. This is an area where children with ASDs often have a significant positive spike. Dougal (see case study, pp. 16–17) has a good understanding of number and could use place value to count large numbers at 9 years of age. He could count dots on a page to 100 if they were arranged in 10s. He can now add and subtract to 100. His number understanding is well ahead of the rest of his profile – all this despite the fact that he cannot speak. However, it is also an area where children can make very little apparent progress, so what they are taught and how they are taught to use it is really quite important.

Les Staves (2001: 1) quotes Professor of Mathematics Ian Stewart: 'The mathematical mind is rooted in the human visual, tactile and motor systems. Counting is based on touch and movement, geometry is visual.' Mathematics is rooted in the senses, so mathematics education in a school for children with SCLD starts with sensory play.

Exploring objects and sensory play

Exploring objects, learning about cause and effect, experimenting with different substances, corn-flour gloop, playdough, sand and water play, exploring **heuristic playboxes**, playing with lego, bricks and toy cars. The important aspects to concentrate on are:

- Focusing attention on the objects/materials (M1).
- Exploring what the object/material can do, how they can change or be changed (M1).
- Joint attention, sharing the objects materials with another, leading to communication about the objects/materials (C3, M13).

Sorting and matching

After exploration comes sorting and matching. It cannot be overemphasised how essential and useful the skills of sorting and matching are. These are real-life skills and matching can be used instead of counting in real-life situations. For example, Class 9 has the job of delivering the milk to the other classes. They work out how much milk is needed, for example, for Class 3 using a matching board. The Class 3 matching board has 6 'shadows' of milk cartons that the cartons are placed on to get the correct number. Sorting and matching are tracked with categorisation in M12 and in M13.

Sorting and matching involves discrimination between same and different, and similar and dissimilar – for example, sorting knives and forks: the forks might not be identical, but they will be similar. Matching and sorting can obviously be practised in box work and group work, but the normal school day offers many real-life examples as well, such as tidying up toys and art materials, fetching cooking implements and laying the table (place mats with cutlery outlines). Sorting and matching skills use the visual and procedural memories. Sorting and matching experiences are closely linked to language and communication, and are linked with in Communication, Language and Literacy in *Learning Tracks*, starting with **object permanence** and developing through to categorisation (M13).

Numbers (M2)

Numbers are mathematical concepts. A mathematical concept is a network of connections between concrete symbols, mathematical symbols, language and pictures. One of the main difficulties of mathematics is that one symbol represents many vastly different situations. Children encounter this difficulty when learning about number. How old are you? What house do you live in? How many sweets do you have? It is very important that a teacher of children with SCLD trying to teach his/her class to count has a very clear idea of what is involved in counting. It is not a simple process; here, task analysis can be useful.

Number has two complementary aspects: *ordinality and cardinality*.

Ordinality (ordinal numbers): the idea that numerals can be used to describe numbers in a sequence – for example, room 3, house number, page 3, 3 o'clock, first, second, third, numbers on a number line.

Cardinality (cardinal numbers): the idea that number names can be used to describe the number of objects in a collection – for example, 3 fingers, 3 houses, 3 unifix bricks, 3 on a dice.

The mathematical relationships underpinning these concepts are ordering and one-to-one correspondence.

Counting (M2)

Ordinality, cardinality, ordering and one-to-one matching come together in counting.
What is involved in counting (task analysis)?

1. The stable order of number sequence when the child learns the number word sequence in the correct order.
2. One number name to each object: the child matches the number words to the objects in a set. As each number word is said, it is being used in an ordinal sense to label the objects and order them.
3. Cardinality: the last number name describes the size of the set and labels the set.

Learning to count

Many children around the world learn to count at an early age, but this does not mean that it is easy, nor is it done quickly. In the United Kingdom, children take about five years to learn to use the first nine numbers.

The process of learning to count involves:

1. Learning the sequence of number names.
2. This takes a lot of practice (many parents fondly believe that their children can count because they have learnt 'the number rhyme'). You have to be able to remember the names and their order, and memory is a big problem for children with SCLD. Nevertheless, this is an area which needs to be engaged in and requires plenty of practice. Through number rhymes and just counting stuff, up and down stairs, bounces on a trampoline, bricks, everything. It can be fun.
3. Attaching one number name to each object of the set to be counted.
4. To do this, children need to be able to:

   a. Remember the number names in the right order.
   b. Count each object once and only once, not count one object twice or forget an object.
   c. Make a one-to-one correspondence between each number word and each object to be counted.

This takes a lot of practice. It requires children to be systematic, maybe moving objects that they have to count and remembering where they started. Start with objects that can be moved, move on to objects/pictures in lines and last of all random groupings that cannot be moved.

Initially, when children count they are inconsistent. The first time they get one answer, the next another. This does not worry them. They do not know which answer is right or maybe think they both are. To further confuse the issue, children with ASDs often do not learn to point in the same way that other children do (**declarative pointing**).

Common errors that children make are pointing at an object but saying nothing, pointing at an object and saying two number names, missing pointing at an object, pointing at an object a second time, or simply waving their finger around generally, saying number names. Children make these errors because they lack a systematic procedure for making sure that everything has been counted once and only once, or because they have problems with one-to-one correspondence or both.

One-to-one correspondence

Piaget gave children this task to demonstrate their understanding of one-to-one correspondence. He showed individual children six little bottles and a tray full of glasses. Piaget then asked the children to 'take off the tray just enough glasses, the same number as there are bottles, one glass for each bottle'. Children around 4–5 years old put out the bottles and glasses as shown in Figure 6.1.

Figure 6.1   Bottles and glasses

The crucial factor seemed to be appearance. If they looked the same, children thought they had the same number. They did not pair one glass to one bottle, they did not use one-to-one correspondence. The same children would have difficulty matching one number name to one object. Understanding of one-to-one correspondence is essential for learning to count and needs a lot of practice. Practice involves lots of matching activities – for example, cups and saucers, boxes to box lids, bowls and spoons, bears to beds.

Understanding cardinality

At first, children count without comprehending any cardinal outcome. If asked 'How many candles are there on the cake?' just after counting the candles on the cake, 2- to 3-year-olds will either recount, or say any number word. It is not that they do not remember the last number word, but that they do not realise that the last number word describes the size of the set. Many 4- to 5-year-olds do realise that the last number name describes the size of the set, but the cardinal meaning is still not mature. They can be misled by appearances – for example, one row of six eggs is more than another row of six egg-cups (Figure 6.2).

Figure 6.2   Eggs and egg-cups

Research into children's ideas about counting demonstrate that even children who can count well do not understand what they are doing it for – that is, they do not realise that they are counting to find out how many objects there are in a set (Munn, 1997). Pre-school children typically thought that it was a social or playful activity; one would guess that this would be true of many children with SCLD. Munn suggests that it is very important to make explicit what we are counting for. Research also indicates that some children understand that the answer to the question 'How many?' is the last number counted, but they do not know why; they have merely learnt it by rote, but have no firm understanding of cardinality.

Conservation of number

It does not matter how the objects are moved or arranged, five is still five and is the same numerosity as any other five. This is the point when all the previous notions come together in the concept of the numberness of number. The child understands one-to-one matching and is not confused when objects are spread out or knocked over. S/he knows there are still the same number of objects even though they may look to take up more space.

Recent research has identified the stages children seem to go through while learning about counting:

1. *Pre-number knower.* At the earliest level, the child makes no distinction between different numerals; if asked to give a set number of objects to a puppet, s/he might give one object or a handful.
2. *One knower.* The next stage, typically at 2½ to 3 years of age, the child only knows that one means one and will give one object to a puppet, but when asked to give more than one gives any number of objects higher than one.
3. *Two knower.* Some months later the child knows two as well.
4. *Three knower.* Some months later three, but if asked to give a number of objects more than three will give a random number (more than three).
5. *Four knower.* As above, for four. These children are referred to as 'subset knowers'. Although they may have memorised the numerals in order to ten, they know the exact meanings for only a subset of those numbers.
6. *Cardinal principle knower.* After some time, often longer than a year, the child's counting performance undergoes a dramatic change. S/he is suddenly able to produce the correct cardinality for five and above all at the same time (usually around 4 years of age; Sarnecka and Carey, 2008).

The concepts of cardinality, ordinality, conservation of number, one-to-one correspondence are all tracked in *Learning Tracks* as well as counting to different numbers.

Learning to count is neither easy nor fast. Some children with SCLD will never learn to count and will have to rely on their carers to set up matching activities to replace counting (as above). Many will learn to count small numbers. Some will rely on subitising for small numbers. Subitising is when you look at a group of things and know how many are there by their appearance; most people do this when playing with dice. There will also be children with SCLD who will learn to count very efficiently but may have little understanding of what it is for – they just love counting. Then there will be children who can both count well and understand the result. Whoever you have in your class, when teaching children with SCLD, because learning to count requires so much practice, you will spend a lot of time counting.

Counting and speech

When children first learn to count they count out loud; indeed, even adults when having difficulty counting tend to count out loud. This makes learning to count more difficult for non-verbal children; they have to internalise counting without counting out loud. Most children at the stage of learning to count will be verbal, but not all. Dougal, as mentioned before in this chapter, understands and uses place value to count, but cannot count out loud as he does not speak; this caused him problems when counting when younger and he lost track more easily.

Counting as a logical systematic process

Counting is a logical systematic process and even if a child does not actually develop the skills to be able to engage in it independently, simply engaging in counting with support gives the learner experience of a logical systematic process. Such experience may help with other logical systematic processes – for example, getting dressed as there is a logical systematic order of dressing.

Number and developmental ages

The majority of developmental ages in this book are taken from *Early Years Outcomes* (DfE, 2013).

Table 6.1   Number and developmental ages

Age	Typical behaviour
Birth–11 months (up to 1 year)	• Notices changes in number of objects/images or sounds in groups of up to 3.
8–20 months	• Develops an awareness of number names through their enjoyment of action rhymes and songs that relate to their experience of numbers. • Has some understanding that things exist even when out of sight.
16–26 months (up to 2 years)	• Knows that things exist, even when out of sight. • Beginning to organise and categorise objects – e.g. putting all the teddy bears together or teddies and cars in separate piles. • Saying some counting word randomly.
22–36 months (up to 3 years)	• Selects a small number of objects from a group when asked – for example, 'Please give me one,' 'Please give me two.' • Recites some number names in sequence. • Creates and experiments with symbols and marks representing ideas of numbers. • Begins to make comparisons between quantities. • Uses some language of quantities, such as 'more' and 'a lot'. • Knows that a group of things changes in quantity when something is added or taken away.
30–50 months (up to 4 years)	• Uses some number names and number language spontaneously. • Uses some number names accurately in play. • Recites number in order to ten. • Knows that numbers identify how many objects are in a set. • Sometimes matches numeral and quantity correctly, etc.

DES 2013

Development age charts are used in *Learning Tracks* as a tool for considering a child's possible level of development. All development charts are based on averages of large numbers of children. They are not used as a labelling device. However, it can be useful for a teacher to know what approximate level of development a child may be functioning at, for three reasons:

1. When a teacher suggests a child's target might be counting up to five objects, given his/her notional developmental age, is it a reasonable target?
2. If a child has a notional developmental age of around 3 years and cannot give one object from a pile of objects, what is the reason? A lack of understanding of the language? Or possibly very little experience of any counting? S/he maybe needs more experience.
3. If a child has a notional developmental age of around 3 years and can count to 100, is this a significant spike?

Most experiential learners will not learn to count. Contextual learners may learn to count up to three, possibly five, but to become a confident counter, a child needs to be able to remember the number names, the order they are in and apply a lot of learning. This would generally happen in the generalised learning phase.

Written numbers: numerals

Numerals are used in many contexts – house numbers, bus numbers, prices, birthday cards. The first step along the way to recognising and using numerals is matching. Some young people may not get any further than matching. Class 9 use matching numerals when they catch the bus to go to the shopping centre. They hold up a card with the correct numeral on it as the bus approaches to make sure that it is the correct bus.

Matching can be done in real-life circumstances as above, box work or in games. Playing with calculators can aid familiarity with numerals and of course there are many computer programs which can help. After matching comes identifying the numeral.

The next step is looking at a numeral, identifying it and counting out the correct number of things. This is best done in practical activities like cooking, but can also be practised in group work, individual box work and on the computer.

The next step is counting a set of objects and finding the correct numeral.

The next step may be tracing, then dot-to-dot, then copying to acquire the skill of writing the numerals. However, this is distinct from using number symbols correctly. To use number symbols appropriately, children must be able to count, remember the numeral shapes, know how to write the numeral shape and above all they must understand cardinality. Until children understand cardinality they will not understand the use of conventional numeral notation (such as in sums). Children usually understand cardinality at a developmental age of around 4 years (DfE, 2013).

All these steps are tracked in *Learning Tracks*.

Number operations (arithmetic/sums) (M3)

Once children have attained some facility with counting and some real familiarity with numbers at least to ten, it will be possible for them to begin to understand number operations (arithmetic). Very few children with SCLD 'do sums'. However, this does not mean that they should not be involved in practical activities involving combining sets of objects and removing objects from sets and counting how many are left. The Scottish Curriculum for Excellence early stage experience and outcome in this area is:

- MNU 0–03a: 'I use practical materials and can "count on and back" to help me to understand addition and subtraction, recording my ideas and solutions in different ways.' (M3)

We have used task analysis to describe a possible list of appropriate experiences to ease tracking. One activity which happens naturally in school is sharing things out, either whole things or fractions of things; this is practical division and fractions (M4).

- MNU 0–07a: 'I can share out a group of items by making smaller groups and can split a whole object into smaller parts.' (M4)

Wright et al. (2006a, 2006b) in their Mathematics Recovery books have analysed children's strategies for arithmetic. Mathematics recovery was developed in Australia, America and the United Kingdom in the 1990s, and is a system of diagnostic interview assessment and teaching based on a set of conceptual stages which they have developed to explain how children acquire knowledge and understanding of number. They offer tried and tested ways of helping children learn 'sums'. They use a lot of language (and this would have to be adapted), but they also use lots of simple practical activities that could be replicated in box work (there is also a CD with the practical materials used in the book). They have developed a learning framework in number which describes stages in arithmetic learning and levels of learning in particular arithmetical skills – for example, forward number word sequencing and backward number word sequencing. The stages are based on strategies that children develop during arithmetic learning.

Stage 0: Emergent counting: Learners cannot count visible items.

Stage 1: Perceptual counting: Learners can count perceived objects, but cannot use information concerning objects in a hidden set. If given a handkerchief hiding two counters and three visible counters, the learners would not be able to work out that there are five counters altogether (contextual or generalised phase).

Stage 2: Figurative counting: Learners can count objects in a hidden set, but then use strategies to count the hidden counters from one and then the perceived counters (generalised phase and above).

Stage 3: Initial counting sequence: Learners use counting on to solve hidden set addition problems and missing number problems such as 6 + x = 8 (generalised phase at applying level and above).

Stage 4: Intermediate number sequence: Learners use count-down strategies to solve missing number problems.

Stage 5: Facile number sequence: Learners use a range of non-counting strategies to solve arithmetic problems – for example, known number facts and knowledge of such concepts that addition is the opposite of subtraction (probably out of the scope of *Learning Tracks*, but certainly at the analysing level of Bloom's taxonomy).

They describe how to assess learners' stages and then give a structured system for teaching arithmetic strategies.

Money (M5)

Money confuses everything. The learner is struggling with learning to count 1, 2, 3 carefully, one number for each object, and we come along and give them an object that is 2p or 5p or 10p – it doesn't seem fair. Money is a very abstract concept, yet it is also a set of very practical real-life objects that most learners with SCLD will handle, it is a problem.

Most learners with SCLD will concentrate on the idea of exchange, exchanging some money for something they want, either in real situations – for example, a class snack, or in play situations such as shopping games and in the outside world. This will need a supportive other to enable them to engage in the very important activity of shopping. All children can play with and sort money, and some will be able to start naming coins.

Time (M6)

Only a few children with SCLD will learn to tell the time on an analogue clock. The average age for learning to tell the time is between 7 and 8 years of age. Despite this, we have included learning to tell the time in *Learning Tracks*. Sometimes, because of particular interests, some do learn the 24-hour clock – for example, Colin (p. 96). However, time is much more than being able to tell the time. It is another difficult and complicated concept and at the same time it is a particularly important issue for children with an ASD. As well as clock reading, it incorporates sequencing, duration of events, and includes hours and minutes, days, weeks and years.

The National Autistic Society explains that people with an ASD have difficulties with organising, sequencing and prioritising, and that this may be because of cognitive function deficits which would lead to a lack of understanding of the concept of time. Definitely, children with an ASD, and many children with SCLD not diagnosed with an ASD, get very stressed if they do not know what is happening, what is happening next, how long something is going to go on for, and transitions are particularly upsetting. It is now common practice in schools and homes of such children to have schedules and timetables to create structure and routine, which remove uncertainty and help to make daily life more predictable, which is all part of the prosthetic environment. These are the most important aspects of time and are tracked in *Learning Tracks* as well as in calendars, seasons, birthdays, and day and night.

Measurement (M1, M7)

Measurement is a practical activity embedded in our everyday life. In *Learning Tracks*, measurement starts with sensory play, develops through big and small, comparison of bigger and smaller and more or less, all under the generic heading of: 'I am developing a sense of size and amount by observing, exploring, using and communicating with others about things in the world around me.'

The next stage is developing the vocabulary of measurement – that is, long/tall, heavy/light, full/empty – both at a receptive level, understanding somebody else's spoken word/sign/symbol, and at an expressive level when the learner uses the vocabulary.

After that, comparing two objects – taller/shorter and ordering. (Developmental age 40–60 months: 'Orders 2 or 3 items by length and 2 items by weight or capacity'; DfE, 2013).

There are basically two different ways in which we can specify or compare quantities:

- Counting: dealing with discrete quantities such as counters, marbles, sweets.
- Measuring: dealing with continuous quantities such as ribbons, milk.

Like counting, measurement is a complicated concept and most of our ideas about the development of children's notions of measurement derive from the work of Piaget (Dickson et al., 1984: 83). The general developmental sequence is:

- Global comparison: when assessment of quantities by children are governed by their perceptions, if it looks bigger it is bigger.
- Conservation of quantity: before any real progress can be made, the child needs to understand and accept that certain properties of the world are effectively invariant.

For example, a quantity of liquid remains the same even when poured into a different shaped container. Such ideas cannot be taught directly but are a matter of conviction and are derived from a great deal of experience of the world. Conservation of quantity is generally developed between the age of 7 and 11, but even in typically developing children there will be 10-year-olds who have not grasped the concept (Hughes, 1981: 87). Most learners with SCLD will not grasp this concept.

- Transitivity: is the idea that if a = b and b = c, then a = c. Acceptance of this is fundamental to the use of units of measurement.
- Standard units: a standard unit of measurement is required in order to communicate with others.

Measurement is, nevertheless, a real-life activity that is engaged in by people with SCLD. They can learn to use measurements by rote or follow visual instructions so as to complete familiar tasks such as cooking. We mark weights needed in cookery on scales. Learners can engage in measuring activities supported by knowledgeable others (scaffolding). Measuring activities which involve matching are easier than ones involving counting – for example, cut a piece of ribbon the same length as another piece of ribbon, not using a ruler – though it can be fun to use non-standard units as a counting exercise.

Patterns and relationships (M8)

Tracking patterns and relationships and symmetry in *Learning Tracks* is mainly based on activities in music, PE and art.

Shape, position and movement (M9)

The young child's first interactions with the environment are almost totally spatial in nature, seeing and touching. Many psychologists – for example, Piaget and Bruner – believe that the manipulation of concrete objects forms the basis of human knowledge and in particular mathematical knowledge. Physical actions become internalised and conceptualised and words become attached to these concepts. Unlike number, there is no clear progression of learning in geometry; the same activities can be approached simultaneously with children with a wide range of abilities.

1. Properties of 2D and 3D objects.

Learning Tracks in this area, tracks learning from:

- exploration of heuristic playboxes through inset puzzles, posting boxes, jigsaw puzzles – all activities that are both visual (our children's strength) and logical and thus very good for developing thinking skills (also good activities for box work);
- naming and using flat shapes and solid shapes;
- using attributes of shape.

2. Angle, symmetry and transformation (M10–11).

This area mainly involves learning about position and direction and is a practical active area of learning best learnt in PE, Forest School and in the playground (H14):

- finding things and people;
- following directions;
- understanding and using positional vocabulary such as 'on', 'in', 'behind' and 'through';
- directing a technological toy.

A favourite drama/PE/mathematics activity is acting out a story like 'We're going on a bear hunt' (Rosen, 1989).

Information handling (M12–13)

This involves collecting objects and information, sorting these objects and displaying the objects/information in different ways, for example bar charts.

Case Study

At school, we often have opinion polls where children and young people make choices by sticking their photo on one side or another of a chart showing the choices – for example, 'What would you like to grow in the tubs in the garden?' with photos of daffodils, wall flowers, hebe bushes ... Then charts are made of the results and shared in assembly.

Conclusion

Mathematics is the smallest of the curriculum sections, but it contains some important learning experiences and outcomes. Many children will not learn to count or engage in mathematical operations because this learning involves the declarative memory. However, with planning, teachers can teach children to use sorting and matching to great effect; and activities like measuring and using timetables can also be learnt practically.

References

Department for Education (DfE) (2013) Early years outcomes (www.gov.uk/government/uploads/system/uploads/attachment_data/file/237249/Early_Years_Outcomes.pdf, accessed 5 October 2015).

Dickson, L., Brown, M. and Gibson, O. (1984) *Children Learning Mathematics*. Oxford: Holt Education.

Hughes, E.R. (1981) A comparative study of the order of acquistion of the concepts of weight, area and volume. In Floyd, A. (ed.) *Developing Mathematical Thinking*. London: Addison-Wesley (p. 87).

Munn, P. (1997) Children's beliefs about counting. In Thompson, I. (ed.) *Teaching and Learning Early Number*. Maidenhead: McGraw-Hill.

National Autistic Society (n.d.) Organising, sequencing and prioritising (www.autism.org.uk/living-with-autism/understanding-behaviour/organising-sequencing-prioritising.aspx, accessed 5 October 2015).

Rosen, M. (1989) *We're Going on a Bear Hunt*. London: Walker.

Sarnecka, B. and Carey, S. (2008) How counting represents number: What children must learn and when they learn it. *Cognition*, 108(3): 662–74.

Staves, L. (2001) *Mathematics for Children with Severe and Profound Learning Difficulties*. London: David Fulton.

Stewart, I. (1997) Royal Institute Christmas lecture. In Staves, L. (2001) *Mathematics for Children with Severe and Profound Learning Difficulties*. London: David Fulton.

Wright, R., Martland, J. and Stafford, A. (2006a) *Early Numeracy Assessment for Teaching and Intervention*. London: Sage.

Wright, R., Martland, J., Stafford, A. and Stanger, G. (2006b) *Teaching Number: Advancing Children's Skills and Strategies*. London: Sage.

PART 3

Using *Learning Tracks*

7

The Framework for Recognising Achievement

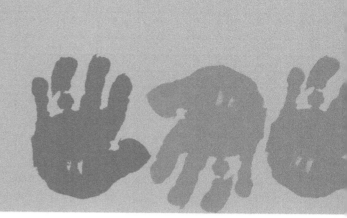

The framework

The framework has been designed to enable the recording of small steps of learning. In the booklet, possible learning steps are organised as Learning Outcomes. For example, in the section below, 'I can make a simple choice from 2' is the Learning Outcome. The Learning Experiences associated with this outcome are listed beneath – for example, 'using behaviour', 'using body language' and 'using VOCA', etc.

Next to each Learning Outcome are boxes labelled from above with the level descriptors of 'Experiential', 'Contextual' and 'Generalised' learning divided into 'Encountering', 'Noticing', 'Responding', and so on.

Next to each Learning Experience is a simple box.

Table 7.1 Framework exemplar

	Experiential			Contextual			Generalised		
	Encountering P1i	Noticing P1ii	Responding P2i	Engaging P2ii	Participating P3i	Communicating P3ii	Remembering P4	Understanding P5, P6	Applying P7, P8
I can make a simple choice from 2									
using behaviour									
using body language									
using gesture									
using eye pointing									
using photo									
using symbol									
using sign									
using my VOCA									
using speech									

Recording learning

Each pupil's learning can be tracked by using an identified colour for the year. These colours should be consistent throughout the school. As this is a black-and-white book, our examples use black, dark grey, light grey and white instead of colours.

A small vertical mark is made on the left side of the appropriate box next to each experience that the pupil has engaged in that year. Once the experiences have been tracked, a decision can then be made about what level they have engaged in these experiences.

For example:

Black = 2011–12; dark grey = 2012–13; light grey = 2013–14; white with black outline = 2014–15.

Table 7.2 Marked framework exemplar

	Experiential			Contextual			Generalised		
	Encountering P1i	Noticing P1ii	Responding P2i	Engaging P2ii	Participating P3i	Communicating P3ii	Remembering P4	Understanding P5, P6	Applying P7, P8
I can make a simple choice from 2		II	I						
using behaviour			III						
using body language									
using gesture									
using eye pointing									
using photo			II						
using symbol			I						
using sign									
using my VOCA									
using speech									

So this learner, over the three years, was consistently able to make choices using behaviour and body language, and has begun to learn to make choices with photos and symbols (boxes next to learning outcomes). At the same time, s/he had progressed in this area from 'Responding' to 'Engaging' in that, although the choice-making may still be heavily supported by adults, this learner has shown more consistent attention and awareness of what in this case is going to happen when s/he hands over a grape symbol.

The use of symbols learning could well have been part of a particular target, but the maintenance of the skill of using body language to make choices probably was not and this is one of the advantages of *Learning Tracks* in that it monitors maintenance of learning and learning outside particular annual targets, and thus gives a better picture of the pupil's achievements rather than simply recording the learning associated with the targets for the year.

When starting to use *Learning Tracks*, we advise using the Development Chart, developed from the Government's Early Years Outcomes 2013, at the back of *Learning Tracks*, to get a feeling for the level the pupil is functioning at in the experiential, contextual or generalised phase. Simply shade on the chart in the colour for the year every activity that you have regularly seen the pupil engage in; this should quickly give an idea of where the child is and demonstrate any spikes or particular deficits in learning. The advice to use the year colour means that another teacher in another year can use the same chart to get a feeling for where the child is functioning, and this will build up another picture of the pupil's development over time.

At our school, we complete the *Learning Tracks* booklet once or twice a year. We fill it in at the end of the year when we know the pupil best. The document is then handed on to the new class team. Some teachers also fill in the document around the time of the pupil's annual review while preparing for planning (in the assigned colour for that academic year).

Annual reviews at our school run from October to Easter. Parents, teachers, therapists and other interested parties meet together to review the pupils learning and plan for the following year's learning. *Learning Tracks* can be useful to demonstrate achievement.

If a school decides to use *Learning Tracks*, they need to work together to create a common understanding of the different levels. This is best done by:

- filling in the development chart for different pupils and discussing;
- by perusing the Exemplar Levels chart in Appendix 1 in the *Learning Tracks* booklet and below;
- filling in *Learning Tracks* in pairs enabling discussion.

The process

If you know your pupil, it should not take long to record his or her achievements for the year. Start at the beginning and make a mark in that year's colour against each Learning Experience you have observed the pupil to engage in regularly that year (planned or unplanned). If you have not

Table 7.3 Exemplar levels table

	Experiential			Engaging P2ii	Contextual		Remembering P4	Generalised	
	Encountering P1i	Noticing P1ii	Responding P2i		Participating P3i	Communicating P3ii		Understanding P5, P6	Applying P7, P8
C3.7 I can communicate No.	Is involved in a range of experiences. May be completely passive. May react in a range of different ways, e.g. running away.	Reacts to experiences in increasingly predictable ways. Staff guess dislikes and model No (gesture, word, sign, symbol) appropriately. Attends briefly to No.	Usually rejects things s/he is known to dislike. More attentive to staff modelling. May attempt a gesture or make an appropriate sound.	Communicates No by gesture or body language. With support can choose correct sign/symbol/word.	Uses No sign/symbol/word in familiar rehearsed situations with encouragement.	Uses no sign/symbol/word in familiar rehearsed situations independently.	Uses sign/symbol/word No in variety of novel situations. Can answer simple yes/no questions in familiar situations.	Answers more complex yes/no questions. E.g. On a story: Does Goldilocks like the wolf?	Understands the consequences of No – If I can't do this, then I have to do that.
C3.13 I can follow a simple instruction, e.g. coat on peg.	Puts coat on peg hand-over-hand support. May be passive or react in a variety of ways.	Puts coat on peg hand over hand. May briefly look at peg or move towards peg more independently.	Still requires complete physical support but shows more awareness, e.g. may hold coat and wait for help.	Begins to follow instruction. When in cloakroom with coat in hand close to peg – can complete the action.	Follows sign/symbol/word instruction in cloakroom with coat and peg – familiar rehearsed situation – with minor prompting.	Follows sign/symbol/word instruction in cloakroom with coat and peg – familiar rehearsed situation. Independently.	Follows the instruction from outside the cloakroom.	Follows the instruction to hang somebody else's coat up on their peg.	Can hang up any coat on any peg in any cloakroom from sign/symbol/word instruction.
C10.2 I can play with an adult, e.g. blowing bubbles.	Present whilst bubbles float around him/her.	Begins to notice bubbles. May eye track or touch a bubble. May choose to remain at activity.	Shows pleasure or displeasure on seeing bubbles. May stay longer at activity.	Shows pleasure and anticipation for bubbles – supported to ask for more – sign/symbol/word (SSW).	Will choose bubbles game. When adult stops making bubbles – asks for more (SSW). Less support – e.g. gestural.	When adult stops making bubbles – asks for more bubbles (SSW). Independently in this familiar rehearsed situation.	Will ask to play bubbles game. Will look for bubbles tube.	N/A	N/A
C10.3 I can share purposeful play with an adult, e.g. build a brick tower and knock it down.	Stays in play space whilst bricks are built up. Knocks down tower hand over hand.	Begins to notice brick tower. May eye track or touch bricks.	Reacts when tower falls down. Picks up a brick.	Attempts a turn to build tower. Knocks tower down – often far too early.	Good turn-taking to build tower. Can wait to knock tower down.	Asks for more bricks. Asks to repeat the activity. May comment on tower falling down.	Will find bricks and ask an adult to play with him/her.	N/A	
H8.1 I can review my learning. H8.1a In the moment.	Is involved in a range of experiences. May be completely passive. May react in a range of different ways, e.g. running away.	Reacts to experiences in increasingly predictable ways. Staff guess dislikes and model like and dislike appropriately. Attends briefly modelling.	Reacts to experiences in increasingly predictable ways. Staff support pupil to sign/symbol say – like/dislike.	Communicates by body language/gesture like and dislike. Supported by staff to choose correct symbol at end of activity.	With support chooses/touches the correct like/dislike symbol at the end of a familiar activity to review activity.	Chooses/touches the correct like/dislike symbol at the end of a familiar activity to review activity.	Communicates feelings about activity. May communicate about previous activities.	May be able to communicate what it was s/he liked/disliked about the activity.	May be able to discuss which activities s/he likes and dislikes generally.
H8.1c In my review sheets.*	Hand over hand.	Hand over hand – might briefly look at the review sheet, particularly if it has photos of self.	More interested in review sheet if it has photos of self.	With support, can stick correct symbol on review sheet (like/dislike).	With minor support (e.g. gestural) can stick correct symbol on review sheet (like/dislike).	Can choose correct symbol for review sheet independently in familiar rehearsed situations.	Can fill in a full review sheet independently.	Can look at review sheets and comment upon whether s/he liked/dislike the activity.	Can make decisions about further work based upon review sheets.

*Review sheets – sheets filled in at the end of an activity reviewing the lesson. Usually individual – photo of child at top, date stamp. Photo of child engaged in activity, then space to stick like/dislike symbol to communicate how pupil felt about activity. Sometimes sent home to parents to communicate work for the day and for child/parent to share work at school that day.

(Continued)

Table 7.3 (Continued)

	Experiential			Contextual				Generalised	
	Encountering P1i	Noticing P1ii	Responding P2i	Engaging P2ii	Participating P3i	Communicating P3ii	Remembering P4	Understanding P5, P6	Applying P7, P8
H11.3 I can dress myself.	Allows adults to undress/dress him/her.	Shows some awareness of being dressed/undressed – may move arms/legs helpfully.	Pushes arms through sleeves, legs through trousers. Holds out feet and hands appropriately.	Actively involved in undressing and dressing routines. Pulling T-shirt over head and pushing foot into shoe.	Puts on tube socks, puts on shoes without fastening – maybe on wrong foot.	Does up easy buttons. Puts on and takes off elasticated trousers. Follows dressing schedule with support.	Dresses and undresses only needing help for fastenings, order and orientation.	Can follow a familiar dressing schedule.	Dresses and undresses independently.
H25.20a I can make a one-course meal, e.g. vegetable soup and toast.	Is present in the kitchen whilst meal is being made, any involvement requires total physical support.	Begins to notice aspects of cooking, e.g. mixer, and may touch utensils and food.	More interested in the activity – may attempt to eat food and engage in activities.	Engages in cooking activities of cutting, stirring, etc. with physical support when necessary.	In familiar and practised situations, participates in all the different aspects of making the meal with gestural and verbal support.	In familiar and practised situations, participates in all the different aspects of making the meal following symbol/spoken instructions.	Uses a developing set of cookery skills appropriately, e.g. using a microwave to prepare a soup and toast.	Can sequence meal-preparing activities with a reasonable degree of accuracy, e.g. answer questions on what to do first.	Uses a repertoire of preparation skills to make a simple one-course meal with minimal supervision.
M2.5 I can count. M2.5a I can point to things one at a time to somebody else counting.	Involved in a range of hand over hand counting activities, e.g. songs and rhymes in intensive interaction.	Notices aspects of the hand-over-hand counting (eye direction).	Shows more interest in counting activities. May touch objects being counted independently.	Engages in random pointing and touching of objects whilst adult says number names.	Participates in a range of counting activities – beginning to understand 1 number name to one object – to adult counting. Possibly learning some number names.	Becoming more skilled at assigning one number name to one object only but needs support to stop once all the objects have been counted.	Counts objects to 3 accurately, i.e. touch each object only once and assign correct number name in correct sequence.	Counts objects to 5 accurately.	Counts objects to 10 accurately.
M6.1 I can use a timetable.	Is present in circle when timetables are discussed. Is shown large timetable photo-symbols	May look briefly at timetable photo-symbols.	May handle and look more carefully at timetable photo-symbols.	Recognises activities on timetable symbols. Puts away timetable symbol when activity finished with physical support.	Looks at timetable at beginning of activity. Puts away symbol at end of activity with verbal and gestural support.	In familiar practised routines, can follow a simple work schedule with minimum supervision. Practised at returning to daily timetable between activities.	Uses a simple work schedule/timetable independently.	Uses a novel work schedule/timetable with minimal support.	Uses all sorts of schedules/timetables in all sorts of situations to manage anxiety.
M13.10 I can categorise/sort. M13.10b I can sort things as part of tidying up, e.g. cutlery in cutlery drawer.	Passively allows staff to engage him/her in handling cutlery.	Begins to notice activity – may handle cutlery by self.	If a spoon is given to him/her – may put it in a box – any box.	Joins in with sorting knives, forks and spoons – but not necessarily accurately.	Makes a good attempt at accurate sorting – may lose concentration, needs support to stay on task.	In familiar rehearsed situation, can complete task.	Can independently put cutlery away appropriately in any cutlery drawer.	Can generalise knife, fork, spoon sorting to any similar 3-way sorting.	
M13.10c I can categorise/sort for one difference, e.g. pictures of animals/transport into boxes.	N/A	N/A	N/A	Looks at pictures, puts in boxes – needs support to choose correct boxes.	Makes good attempt at accurate sorting – may need support to maintain focus.	In familiar rehearsed situations, can complete the task independently.	Can sort novel objects into 2 sets.		
M13.10g I can categorise/sort for 2 differences, e.g. big/small cars/boats.	N/A	N/A	N/A	N/A	N/A	Attempts task but needs support.	After much practice, can complete the task with minimal support.	In familiar rehearsed situations, can complete the task independently.	Can sort novel objects by 2 differences.

◼ Experiential learning   ⊠ Contextual learning   ⸬ Generalised learning

observed the pupil engage in a Learning Experience, leave the box blank. It may be that you *think* s/he can do something; however, if you have not observed it, do not mark it. Occasionally, you may feel that you need to make further observations, but generally the idea is that you record what you have seen on multiple occasions, so there should be little confusion.

The next step is trickier but will become easier the more you do it. Go back to the Learning Outcome at the top of the Learning Experiences and make a judgement at what level s/he engaged in the Learning Outcome. To help you make these decisions, refer back to the learner's Development Chart (at the back of the accompanying booklet – it is best to fill this in *every* year before you start recording), study Table 7.3, the Exemplar levels chart, and discuss your thinking with colleagues. The important thing is that teachers in a school come to a common agreement about what the different level descriptors mean and this will take time. Sadly, assessing learning is not like weighing vegetables. It is an inexact science and these level descriptors are designed to distinguish between small increments of learning. Our advice at the beginning is be conservative and be careful not to be over-positive about achievement. It is a teacher's tendency (and even more so support staff) to inflate children's achievements, which may be positive when discussing achievement with parents, but not so positive if you are plotting learning over several years. If you begin by overestimating achievement, you will have no progress to plot, which can be disheartening. It will take a few years to settle into agreement about the levels, and new teachers to the school will have to be supported in their early engagement with *Learning Tracks*. Mistakes will be made, but over the course of the years a pupil's pattern of learning will be built up.

Planning for learning

Usually, while filling in or reviewing *Learning Tracks,* teachers get ideas about what the next steps for pupils might be. These possibilities can be taken to the review or discussed with parents before the review, and with the pupil if appropriate.

In Standards and Expectations, it was emphasised that pupils could make progress in one of three ways:

- By achieving a breadth of learning through an increasing wide range of experiences that is within the outcome planning for one of the other experiences.
- By responding to the level of the challenge by becoming increasingly independent. If they have achieved a learning experience at the engagement level, their next target would be to work at it at the participation level (each level is increasingly independent).
- By applying what they have learnt in a range of contexts, the above two remain the same and the experience is just done somewhere else. Pupils with an ASD find this type of target particularly challenging. Some of the Learning Experiences list the different situations – for example, I can use sign in a range of situations at snack, choices and lunch.

The language of *Learning Tracks* can be used to link it with the planning document:

… will encounter situations where …

… will notice/be aware of …

… will respond to …

… will engage in activities where …

… will participate in activities where …

… will communicate about …

… will remember information/vocabulary/processes related to …

… will understand information/vocabulary/processes related to …

… will apply skills and knowledge related to …

☐ Experiential learning   ☒ Contextual learning   ☐ Generalised learning

If teachers throughout the school agree to use the same language, it can make planning documents look more professional. However, it is not necessary and it doesn't always make sense.

Example case studies

These case studies give examples of recording and planning using *Learning Tracks*. The cases include three of our case study children from the chapter on Case Studies and two younger children. The colours used for recording are: 2011–2012 (black); 2012–2013 (dark grey); 2013–2014 (light grey); and 2014–2015 (white outlined).

Case study

Donald: Long-term Learning Outcomes for 2014–2015

Donald has six long-term Learning Outcomes in 2014–2015. The structure of this case study is:

a. each area of learning is introduced by a description of Donald's achievements
b. demonstrated by his *Learning Tracks* record in that area up to 2014, which then leads on to
c. his new Long-term Learning Outcome (LtLO).

Long-term Learning Outcome 1

a. Donald uses speech but he is dyspraxic and his speech is unclear; a VOCA or tablet/iPad would be a very useful back-up for Donald, but his dyspraxia and general impatience rules that out at the moment. Donald was assessed by a speech and language therapist to analyse what could support his communication. A pointing book was identified (has lots of pictures of things that can be pointed to). However, many of the things that he wants to communicate about are simply not in the books – for example, 'X factor', so it was decided he needed help with his articulation.
b. Table 7.4 shows Donald's *Learning Tracks* record.

Table 7.4   Donald's *Learning Tracks* record to the end of the academic year 2013–2014 (1)

	Experiential			Contextual			Generalised		
	Encountering P1i	Noticing P1ii	Responding P2i	Engaging P2ii	Participating P3i	Communicating P3ii	Remembering P4	Understanding P5, P6	Applying P7, P8
I can make meaningful vocalisations			**I**	**I I**					
a I can copy sounds		**I I I**							
b I can join in with action songs		**I I I**							
c I can make myself understood to familiar listeners using speech		**I I**							
d I can make myself understood to unfamiliar listeners using speech									

c. New LtLO 'Donald will participate in exercises to articulate sounds more clearly' (LIT 0–01a/LIT 0–11a/Lit0–20a).

Long-term Learning Outcome 2

a. As a result of his ASD, attachment disorder and SLD, Donald gets very anxious. Timetables and work schedules give him a lot of support. He needs to develop his ability to understand, use and talk about his timetables.

b. Table 7.5 shows Donald's *Learning Tracks* record.

Table 7.5   Donald's *Learning Tracks* record to the end of the academic year 2013–2014 (2)

	Experiential			Contextual			Generalised		
	Encountering P1i	Noticing P1ii	Responding P2i	Engaging P2ii	Participating P3i	Communicating P3ii	Remembering P4	Understanding P5, P6	Applying P7, P8
I can use a timetable				**I**	**I**	I			
a I can understand object signifiers for my timetable			**I**						
b I can use a symbol timetable			**III**						

c. New LtLO 'Donald will communicate about following a varied daily timetable with visual supports for each session' (LIT 0–04a/LIT 0–14a).

You will note that the target is at the level at which he is functioning, which is in line with guidance in Standards and Expectations, both:

- achieving breadth of learning through an increasing range of experiences; and
- applying what he is learning in a range of contexts.

Long-term Learning Outcome 3

a. Donald is very good at greeting people; he greets everybody with the same degree of familiarity and enthusiasm; this is not unusual for a child with attachment disorder. However, he does need to learn to be more circumspect with strangers.
b. Table 7.6 shows Donald's *Learning Tracks* record.

Table 7.6   Donald's *Learning Tracks* record to the end of the academic year 2013–2014 (3)

		Experiential			Contextual			Generalised		
		Encountering P1i	Noticing P1ii	Responding P2i	Engaging P2ii	Participating P3i	Communicating P3ii	Remembering P4	Understanding P5, P6	Applying P7, P8
Part 6										
I can initiate a greeting								**I**	**II**	
a To a familiar person	1:1			**III**						
	In circle			**III**						
	In school			**III**						
	In the community			**III**						
b To an unfamiliar person	1:1			**III**						
	In circle			**III**						
	In school			**III**						
	In the community			**III**						

Donald has problems with greeting strangers – he greets everybody

c. New LtLO 'Donald will participate in activities to learn about strangers and appropriate greetings' (HWB 0–14a).

Here, Donald's *Learning Tracks* records that he is at a generalised phase of understanding greetings, which in many ways he is. Nevertheless, he lacks the understanding of *who* to greet. *Learning Tracks* is simply not sophisticated enough to deal with all eventualities. Donald is unusual in our school; most of our pupils are very circumspect around strangers, so our solution is to make a small handwritten comment in the booklet and to write an appropriate target. Another school may wish to add appropriate experiences and outcomes.

Long-term Learning Outcome 4

a. Donald finds being out and about in the community frightening, especially new situations. Nevertheless, with the correct supports he is extending places he will go to.

b. Table 7.7 shows Donald's *Learning Tracks* record.

Table 7.7 Donald's *Learning Tracks* record to the end of the academic year 2013–2014 (4)

	Experiential			Contextual			Generalised		
	Encountering P1i	Noticing P1ii	Responding P2i	Engaging P2ii	Participating P3i	Communicating P3ii	Remembering P4	Understanding P5, P6	Applying P7, P8
I can join in the wider community (cinema, cafe, etc.)			❚❚	❙					
a supermarket		❚❚❙							
b cafe		❙							
c theatre		❙							
d cinema		❙							
e									
f									

c. New LtLO 'Donald will participate weekly in varied situations in the community with visual supports' (HWB 0–13a).

Long-term Learning Outcome 5

a. Donald has a good understanding of money (see Figures 7.1 and 7.2).

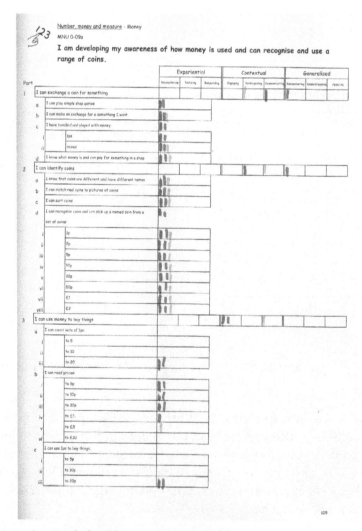

Figure 7.1   Donald's *Learning Tracks* booklet – money pages (1)

Figure 7.2   Donald's *Learning Tracks* booklet – money pages (2)

He can use money to buy things at a participating level, with quite a lot of support. He needs to engage in plenty of shopping situations (real, in group work and box work) so that he becomes 'well rehearsed' and thus more confident to pay for things more independently.

b. Table 7.8 shows Donald's *Learning Tracks* record.

Table 7.8   Donald's *Learning Tracks* record to the end of the academic year 2013–2014 (5)

	Experiential			Contextual			Generalised		
	Encountering	Noticing	Responding	Engaging	Participating	Communicating	Remembering	Understanding	Applying
	P1i	P1ii	P2i	P2ii	P3i	P3ii	P4	P5, P6	P7, P8
I can use money to buy things				❚❚	▓				

c. New LtLO 'Donald will communicate in activities choosing different coins to pay for things' (MNU0–09a).

Long-term Learning Outcome 6

a. Donald has a good understanding of the use of timetables, but he needs to develop his feeling for time throughout the day to further develop his use of timetables, which really are critical to his life; part of his prosthetic environment.

b. Table 7.9 shows Donald's *Learning Tracks* record.

Table 7.9   Donald's *Learning Tracks* record to the end of the academic year 2013–2014 (6)

		Experiential			Contextual			Generalised		
		Encountering	Noticing	Responding	Engaging	Participating	Communicating	Remembering	Understanding	Applying
		P1i	P1ii	P2i	P2ii	P3i	P3ii	P4	P5, P6	P7, P8
I can understand and use key times of the day					❚❚	▓				
a	I understand day and night		❚❚❚							
b	I can sort things that happen in the day and night		❚▓							

(Continued)

Table 7.9   (Continued)

		Experiential			Contextual			Generalised	
		Encountering	Noticing	Responding	Engaging	Participating	Communicating	Remembering	Understanding	Applying
		P1i	P1ii	P2i	P2ii	P3i	P3ii	P4	P5, P6	P7, P8
c	I understand morning and afternoon (DA 4yrs)		▌							
d	I can point to morning and afternoon activities on the timetable									

c. New LtLO 'Donald will communicate in activities to develop his knowledge of time in relation to key parts of his day' (MNU0–010a).

These are Donald's key targets for 2015. They are in no way the sum of his learning for the year. IEPs, CSPs, EHCs only plan for key targets. *Learning Tracks*, on the other hand, records a much wider range of learning, which gives a clearer picture of the whole child. For example, although reading is not one of his targets, Donald is continuing to learn to read in his box work and other experiences around the school and community. His reading development will continue to be recorded in *Learning Tracks*. A subsequent teacher may feel that his reading is a priority and will be able to pick up the level he is at and what would be an appropriate target from *Learning Tracks*, despite the fact that he may not have had a reading target for three years.

Case Study

Andrew: Long-term Learning Outcomes for 2013–2014

The structure of this case study is:

a. Andrew's old Long-term Learning Outcomes (LtLO) for 2013–2014.
b. His *Learning Tracks* record up to the end of the academic year 2014–2015.
c. A comment on his progress.

Long-term Learning Outcome 1

Andrew is a non-verbal young person who is learning to use symbols to communicate. In the year 2012–2013, he exhibited a sudden regression which lasted for 18 months – a long enough period of time to be noted in *Learning Tracks*, normal progression would be a black mark, followed by a dark grey mark and then a light grey mark; his is dark-grey, black, light-grey. Fortunately, he seems on track again. Most of his communication skills are judged to be at the engaging level, which has a very high level of adult support. His long-term learning outcome for last year was:

a. Old LtLO1 'Andrew will participate in using PECS by discriminating between a range of symbols to make requests throughout the day' (LIT 0–10a).
b. Table 7.10 shows Andrew's *Learning Tracks* record (1).

Table 7.10   Andrew's *Learning Tracks* record for the end of the 2014–2015 academic year (1)

		Experiential			Contextual			Generalised	
		Encountering	Noticing	Responding	Engaging	Participating	Communicating	Remembering	Understanding	Applying
		P1i	P1ii	P2i	P2ii	P3i	P3ii	P4	P5, P6	P7, P8
I can make requests			▌		▌▌	▯				
a	I can request by eye pointing									
b	I can hand over a symbol to get something I want (PECS phase1)	▌▌▯								
c	I can request by sign									
d	I can request by VOCA									
e	I can request verbally									

	Experiential			Contextual			Generalised		
	Encountering P1i	Noticing P1ii	Responding P2i	Engaging P2ii	Participating P3i	Communicating P3ii	Remembering P4	Understanding P5, P6	Applying P7, P8
I can persist to hand over a symbol at increasing distance (PECS phase 2)		■	■	▨	□				
I can travel to get my PECS book/symbol (PECS phase 2)		■	■	▨	□				
I can discriminate between symbols to get what I want (PECS phase 3)		■	■	▨	□				
a 2 symbols									
b 3 symbols									
c 5 symbols									
d 10 symbols		■■▨							
e more		■▨							
I understand the following have meaning:									
a objects of reference				□	□				
b photos			■■	▨	□				
c symbols			■■	▨	□				
d signs			■	▨					
e words		■	■						
f texts									
I can use a single ... within a routine:									
a objects of reference				□					
b symbols		■	■▨	□					
c signs									
d VOCA words									
e spoken words									
f written words (text)									
I can use PECS in a range of situations		■	■▨	□					
a snack			■■■□						
b choices			■■■□						
c lunch			■■□						
d playroom									
e playtime			■■□						
f work			■■■□						
g community			■■□						
h other			■■■□						

c. His teacher believed that he was ready for this step, as a target has to be achievable. In practice, Andrew was expected to do what he was already doing with less adult support. Andrew is making wonderful progress with his PECS; he really understands the function of this communication, that if he asks for something he will get it, and he is using it at home.

Long-term Learning Outcome 2

Andrew has been working with symbol timetables and work schedules for many years, gradually understanding them more and finding them more useful in terms of reducing anxiety. Again, you can see the regression. His second Communication, Language and Literacy target was:

a. Old LtLO 2 'Andrew will participate in following a varied timetable with increasing independence' (LIT 0–14a).
b. Table 7.11 shows Andrew's *Learning Tracks* record (2).

Table 7.11   Andrew's *Learning Tracks* record for the end of the 2014–2015 academic year (2)

	Experiential			Contextual			Generalised		
	Encountering P1i	Noticing P1ii	Responding P2i	Engaging P2ii	Participating P3i	Communicating P3ii	Remembering P4	Understanding P5, P6	Applying P7, P8
I can use a timetable		▮		▮▮	▯				
a I can understand object signifiers for my timetable									
b I can use a symbol timetable	▮▮▮▯								

c. Again, the target was about less support and more independence. The use of the word 'participate', which is under the heading Contextual Learning, gives a clear indication of the level of this target. Andrew worked in 'familiar rehearsed contexts' with adult support at the level of encouragement to start a task, to stay on task and to get back to the task if he lost concentration. Andrew has gained more understanding of timetables, and one of the ways he demonstrated this was by whacking the timetable when it showed something he did not want to do.

Long-term Learning Outcome 3

Table 7.12   Andrew's *Learning Tracks* record for the end of the 2014–2015 academic year (3)

	Experiential			Contextual			Generalised		
	Encountering P1i	Noticing P1ii	Responding P2i	Engaging P2ii	Participating P3i	Communicating P3ii	Remembering P4	Understanding P5, P6	Applying P7, P8
I can join in circle activities		▮▮▮							
I can join in assembly	▮▮								
I can share in assembly	▮▮								
I can join in the wider community (cinema, cafe, etc.)			▮▮	▯					
a supermarket		▯							
b cafe		▮▮▯							
c theatre		▮▮▯							
d cinema		▯							
e Meadows park		▮▯							
f									

a. Old LtLO 3 'Andrew will engage in varied situations with visual supports' (HWB 0–12a).
b. Table 7.12 shows Andrew's *Learning Tracks* record (3).
c. Again, notice that Andrew engaged in very little 2012–2013, but he is managing to go out in the community again with plenty of support from adults and photographs of where he is going.

Table 7.13   Andrew's *Learning Tracks* record for the end of the 2014–2015 academic year (4)

	Experiential			Contextual			Generalised		
	Encountering P1i	Noticing P1ii	Responding P2i	Engaging P2ii	Participating P3i	Communicating P3ii	Remembering P4	Understanding P5, P6	Applying P7, P8
Toileting – training begins at DA 2+ yrs certainly by DA 3years. Using the toilet independently DA 4–6 yrs									
I can manage my toileting (pee) except for accidents		▮		▮▮	▯				
I can manage my toileting (poo) except for accidents			▮	▮▮▯					

Long-term Learning Outcome 4

a. Old LtLO 4 'Andrew will participate in his toileting routine with increasing independence' (HWB 0–33a).
b. Table 7.13 shows Andrew's *Learning Tracks* record (4).
c. Andrews's toilet-training is back on track. He is asking to pee. Poo is more of a problem due to severe constipation.

Long-term Learning Outcome 5

Andrew cannot count, but he is very good at sorting and matching in familiar rehearsed contexts which are very important mathematical skills that can be used in place of counting.

Table 7.14   Andrew's *Learning Tracks* record for the end of the 2014–2015 academic year (5)

	Experiential			Contextual			Generalised		
	Encountering P1i	Noticing P1ii	Responding P2i	Engaging P2ii	Participating P3i	Communicating P3ii	Remembering P4	Understanding P5, P6	Applying P7, P8
I can categorise/sort		▮	▮		▮□				
a I can sort by colour		▮▮▯□							
b I can sort as part of tidying up, e.g. cutlery in trays		▮▮▯□							
c I can categorise/sort for one difference/attribute with objects (balls cars)		▮▮							
d I can categorise/sort for one difference/attribute (major) pictures/symbols, e.g. transport/animals into boxes/set rings		▮▮▯□							
e I can categorise/sort for one difference/attribute (major) pictures/symbols onto category boards		▮▮▯□							
I can match		▮	▮	▮	□				
a I can match objects that are the same		▮▮▯□							
b I can match photos that are the same		▮▮▯□							
c I can match symbols that are the same		▮▮▯□							
d I can match photos to objects/places		▮□							
e I can match symbols to objects/places		▮□							
f I can match photos to symbols									

a. Old LtLO 5 'Andrew will engage in using his sorting and matching skills for functional life skills.'

Why *engaging* when he has achieved *participation*? Because he is using the skills in new situations, he will not be able to *participate* again until he is familiar with the functional situations.

b. Table 7.14 shows Andrew's *Learning Tracks* record (5).
c. 2015: Andrew has now achieved participation and is using sorting in a range of practical contexts for example laundry.

Case Study

Shona's Long-term Learning Outcomes for 2014 and 2015

Shona is in her second year at school (in class 2).
The structure of this case study is:

a. Shona's 2014 Long-term Learning Outcome (LtLO). The old target.
b. Her *Learning Tracks* record for that area up to the end of the 2013-2014 academic year.

c. A comment on her achievements.

d. Her 2015 Long-term Learning Outcome. The new target.

In this case study, her class 1 teacher uses *Learning Tracks* to inform her choice of targets but does not use the vocabulary of the level descriptors.

Table 7.15   Shona's *Learning Tracks* record for the end of 2013–2014 (1)

	Experiential			Contextual			Generalised		
	Encountering P1i	Noticing P1ii	Responding P2i	Engaging P2ii	Participating P3i	Communicating P3ii	Remembering P4	Understanding P5, P6	Applying P7, P8
I can use eye pointing in a range of situations		▮							
a snack		▮							
b choices									
c lunch		▮							
d playroom		▮							
e playtime		▮							
f work									
g community									
h other									
I can use PECs in a range of situations			▮						
a snack		▮							
b choices		▮							
c lunch									
d playroom									
e playtime									
f work									
g community									
h other									

Long-term Learning Outcome 1

a. Old LtlO 1, 2014: 'I will develop the ability to effectively communicate my choices and requests to another person' (Lit 0–10a).

b. Table 7.15 shows Shona's *Learning Tracks* record (1).

c. Shona was using a PECS book with large photographs for choosing items at snack and choosing time. Unfortunately, this became problematic due to her impulse to throw both the photos and the book. Shona's teacher, in collaboration with her mum, made a **communication book**, an A5 ring-binder with four photos of snack items, toys or activities on each page. Shona recognised the book (she had a similar one at home) and quickly became able to search through it and point at what she wanted. Sadly, Shona has periodical health problems and this has affected her recent progress. She has been less able to focus her communication book, so this year's target is the same as last year's.

Table 7.16   Shona's *Learning Tracks* record for the end of 2013–2014 (2)

		Experiential			Contextual			Generalised		
		Encountering P1i	Noticing P1ii	Responding P2i	Engaging P2ii	Participating P3i	Communicating P3ii	Remembering P4	Understanding P5, P6	Applying P7, P8
I can attend to some who is communicating with me				▮						
a	I can begin to show awareness of people around me		▮							
b	I can distinguish between familiar and unfamiliar people		▮							
c	I can give visual attention to a familiar adult, object or situation									
	i prompted		▮							
	ii unprompted		▮							

		Experiential			Contextual			Generalised		
		Encountering P1i	Noticing P1ii	Responding P2i	Engaging P2ii	Participating P3i	Communicating P3ii	Remembering P4	Understanding P5, P6	Applying P7, P8
d	I can watch a familiar adult's face when they are speaking to me		▨							
e	I can respond to a greeting									
From a familiar person	1:1		▨							
	In circle		▨							
	In school									
	In the community									
From an unfamiliar person	1:1		▨							
	In circle									
	In school									
	In the community									
f	I can give eye contact		▨							
g	I can smile in response to another person smiling									
I can respond using my preferred form of communication when spoken to				▨						
a	I can intentionally react to a familiar person									

d. New LtLO 1, 2015: 'I will continue to develop the ability to effectively communicate my choices and requests to another person.'

Long-term Learning Outcome 2

a. Old LtLO 2, 2014: 'Using a range of strategies, I will build on my social communication skills' (Lit 0–02a).

b. Table 7.16 shows Shona's *Learning Tracks* record (2).

c. Shona's class work is on social skills in circle. Shona is functioning at an experiential phase. It is often difficult to persuade children at an experiential phase to engage in social occasions like circle, but you need social occasions to work on social communication. For a period of time, Shona regularly removed herself from circle and this resulted in her requiring more support than previously to participate in greetings. Happily, she is now choosing to come to circle most of the time and is participating in greetings and choosing activities. The class team hope that if they continue to offer fun and motivating activities at circle, Shona will continue to want to participate and this will help her progress in social communication.

d. New LtLO 2, 2015: Her target remains the same: 'Using a range of strategies, I will build on my social communication skills' (Lit 0–02a).

Table 7.17 Shona's *Learning Tracks* record for the end of 2013–2014 (3)

		Experiential			Contextual			Generalised		
		Encountering P1i	Noticing P1ii	Responding P2i	Engaging P2ii	Participating P3i	Communicating P3ii	Remembering P4	Understanding P5, P6	Applying P7, P8
I can use a timetable				▨						
a	I can show some anticipation of an activity in familiar situations		▨							
b	I understand the sign 'time for'		▨							
c	I understand and respond to simple routines I know		▨							
d	I understand and can use the sign 'finished'									
e	I can understand and use ... for activities									
i	objects of reference									
ii	photos		▨							
iii	symbols									
iv	text									

(Continued)

Table 7.17   (Continued)

	Experiential			Contextual			Generalised		
	Encountering P1i	Noticing P1ii	Responding P2i	Engaging P2ii	Participating P3i	Communicating P3ii	Remembering P4	Understanding P5, P6	Applying P7, P8
f I can match familiar timetable symbols									
g I can take a symbol down from a timetable when I have done the work			▪						
h I know what to do next from a simple timetable strip			▪						
i I can manage transitions									
j I can manage my time using a timetable									
h I can manage my work using a work schedule									
i I can follow a dressing timetable/schedule									

Long-term Learning Outcomes 3 and 4

a. Old LtLO 3, 2014: 'With support, I will learn strategies I can use to help me make transitions in my day' (HWB 0–4a).

This is linked to Learning Outcome 4. These Health and Wellbeing experiences and outcomes are listed in M6. Old LtLO 4, 2014: 'I will use a visual timetable to help me understand what is happening now and next' (MNU 0–10a).

b. Table 7.17 shows Shona's *Learning Tracks* record (3).
c. Review of Learning Outcome 3: Shona has made great progress with transitions around the school this year, with the exception of going out to play, which she really does not enjoy (the class team are working on making playtime more motivating for her).
d. New LtLO 3, 2015: 'I can make transitions in my day with less support, using familiar and new strategies' (HWB 0–4a).

Shona has made progress; the new target is a 'next step'. At St Crispin's we are still developing the use of *Learning Track*, so we are experimenting with the language. Teachers are free to use the language they prefer. In this case, using the tracking descriptors (encounter, notice, respond, etc.) might give a clearer indication of progress.

So the first target could have been:

'Shona will respond to transitions throughout the day' (implying all the relevant support for this level).

And the second target:

'Shona will engage in transitions throughout the day' (implying less support).

Table 7.18   Shona's *Learning Tracks* record for the end of 2013–2014 (4)

	Experiential			Contextual			Generalised		
	Encountering P1i	Noticing P1ii	Responding P2i	Engaging P2ii	Participating P3i	Communicating P3ii	Remembering P4	Understanding P5, P6	Applying P7, P8
I can undress myself				▪					
a I can pull my clothing off my hands			▪						
b I can pull clothing off my feet			▪						
c I can take my arms out of my clothing			▪						
d I can push trousers and pants down			▪						
e I can remove garments with an elasticated waist			▪						
f I can pull clothing over my head			▪						
g I can unbutton a button									

Shona can strip – working on appropriate timing

c. Review of Learning Outcome 4: Shona uses her now and next timetable consistently and demonstrates her understanding of the photographs by leading a member of staff to the door or to the table, or by throwing away photos of things she doesn't want to do. She also looks hard at the photos in circle that tell her the sequence of her whole day and her teacher feels that this routine gives her insight into the structure of her day.

d. New LtLO 4, 2015: 'I will use an extended visual timetable to help me understand what is happening now, next and later' (MNU 10a).

Long-term Learning Outcome 5

a. Old LtLO 5, 2014: 'I will work towards being able to undress independently' (HWB 0–015a).
b. Table 7.18 shows Shona's *Learning Tracks* record (4).

Table 7.19   Shona's *Learning Tracks* record for the end of 2013–2014 (5)

		Experiential			Contextual			Generalised		
		Encountering P1i	Noticing P1ii	Responding P2i	Engaging P2ii	Participating P3i	Communicating P3ii	Remembering P4	Understanding P5,6	Applying P7,8
	I can use shapes to solve a problem			▌						
a	I can complete a form board/inset puzzle	▌								
i	1 piece	▌								
ii	2 pieces	▌								
iii	3–5 pieces									
iv	6–10 pieces									
v	more									
b	I can use a posting box	▌								
i	1 piece	▌								
ii	2 pieces	▌								
iii	3–5 pieces	▌								
iv	6–10 pieces	▌								
v	more	▌								
c	I can do a jigsaw on the big-screen computer									
i	4 pieces									
ii	9 pieces									
iii	16 pieces									
d	I can do a jigsaw									
i	2 pieces	▌								
ii	4–6 pieces (DA 4–5 yrs)									
iii	9–16 pieces									
iv	more									

The little handwritten note prompted us to add 'keeping clothes on' into *Learning Tracks*.

c. Shona is able to undress with little support and is encouraged to be as independent as possible in this task every swimming time. She finds dressing more challenging. She will assist in each stage of dressing but needs support to initiate the next step. Her class team are continuing to use strategies such as **backward chaining** to encourage Shona to be more independent in dressing.

d. New LtLO 5, 2015: 'I will work towards being able to dress independently' (HWB0–15a).

Long-term Learning Outcome 6

a. Old LtLO 6, 2014: 'I will carry out a sequence of tasks from my workbox' (MNU 0–20b and MNU 0–16a).

Matching and sorting are listed M9 and M20.

b. Table 7.19 shows Shona's *Learning Tracks* record (5).

c. Shona very much enjoys workbox time and will regularly sit for half an hour completing motivating and challenging tasks. She enjoys quite difficult puzzles with no matching colours for support and likes sorting shapes and colours. She is clearly making progress and ready to move onto a next level.

d. New LtLO 6, 2015: 'I will carry out a sequence of motivating tasks from my workbox' (MNU 0–20b and MNU 0–16a).

Here, the teachers would definitely benefit from using level descriptors:

2014: 'Shona will respond to a sequence of workbox tasks.'

2015 'Shona will engage with a sequence of workbox tasks.'

These targets clearly demonstrate progression.

Case Study

Jamie's Long-term Learning Outcomes for 2013, 2014 and 2015

Jamie is 9 years old. He is in class 4, where he has been for two years. He is learning within the experiential phase.

The structure of this case study is:

a. Some of Jamie's old Long-term Learning Outcomes for 2013–2014.

b. Beneath some of these Long-term Learning Outcomes we have listed some Short-term Learning Outcomes. All pupils have short-term outcomes as well as long-term outcomes. Some short-term outcomes come directly from *Learning Tracks*, others do not. *Learning Tracks* does not cover everything; if it did, it would be encyclopaedic and unmanageable.

Table 7.20   Jamie's *Learning Tracks* record for the end of 2013–2014 (1)

	Experiential			Contextual			Generalised		
	Encountering P1i	Noticing P1ii	Responding P2i	Engaging P2ii	Participating P3i	Communicating P3ii	Remembering P4	Understanding P5, P6	Applying P7, P8
I can make requests	I	I	I						
a I can request by eye pointing		III							
b I can hand over a symbol to get something I want (PECS phase 1)		II							
c I can request by sign									
d I can request by VOCA									
e I can request verbally									
I can persist to hand over a symbol at increasing distance (PECS phase 2)		I							
I can travel to get my PECS book and travel to hand over a symbol (PECS phase 2)		I							
I can discriminate between symbols to get what I want (PECS phase 3)		II							
a 2 symbols		II							
b 3 symbols		I							
c 5 symbols									

c. Jamie's *Learning Tracks* record of the relevant areas up to the end of the 2013–2014 academic year.

d. Jamie's New Long-term Learning Outcomes for 2015.

Long-term Learning Outcome: Communication, Language and Literacy example 1

a. Old LtLO, 2013: 'I can anticipate events from sounds and visual cues' (LIT 0–01a/LIT 0–11a/ LIT 0–20a).

Old LtLO, 2013: 'I can use PECS to make meaningful choices and requests' (LIT 0–09a).

Old LtLO, 2014: 'I can respond to information and make a request' (LIT 0–10a).

b. 'I can persist to hand over a symbol at increasing distance' (PECS, Phase 2).

  'I can travel to get my PECS book/ symbol and hand over a symbol' (PECS, Phase 2).

c. Table 7.20 shows Jamie's *Learning Tracks* record (1).

Jamie has made good progress with his requesting. When he is focused, he can be very determined and this includes travelling some distance to ensure that a staff member is aware of his request. His discrimination of different symbols remains inconsistent. He will need a lot of practice of requesting with this level of support before he is ready to move on to the engaging level, so his teacher decides to move sideways for the next target. This does not mean that Jamie will not be working on requesting. He will continue to work on it, but it might not be a formal target again until he is ready to work towards engaging.

  In 2015 he has a target for interaction. The advantage of *Learning Tracks* is that it records a range of learning, not only the planned Learning Outcomes, so his 2015 LtLO is based upon evidence of learning and is therefore appropriate.

Table 7.21 Jamie's *Learning Tracks* record on interaction up to the end of 2013–2014

	Experiential			Contextual			Generalised		
	Encountering P1i	Noticing P1ii	Responding P2i	Engaging P2ii	Participating P3i	Communicating P3ii	Remembering P4	Understanding P5, P6	Applying P7, P8
I can take my turn in an interaction	I	II							
a I can be involved in intensive interaction		II							
b I can react briefly towards familiar people, objects and situations		III							
c I can enjoy physical interaction		III							
d I can engage in simple routines in intensive interaction		III							
e I enjoy rough-and-tumble play		III							
f I can join in a chasing game		III							
g I can anticipate a well-practised routine		III							
h I can imitate an adult									
i I can initiate a routine in intensive interaction									

c. Table 7.21 shows Jamie's *Learning Tracks* record on interaction.

d. New LtLO, 2015: 'I can respond to staff and peers who are interacting with me' (LIT 0–02a/ ENG 0–03a).

  • 'I join in with an adult playing with items.'
  • 'I can share purposeful play with an adult.'

Long-term Learning Outcome: Communication, Language and Literacy example 2

a. Old LtLO, 2014: 'I can respond to opportunities to make my opinion known' (LIT 0–02a/ ENG 0–03a).

b.

  • 'I can communicate "yes" using gesture and/or symbol.'
  • 'I can communicate "no" using gesture and/or symbol.'
  • 'I can communicate whether I like an activity or not by pointing at the relevant symbol.'

c. Table 7.22 shows Jamie's *Learning Tracks* record (2).

Table 7.22   Jamie's *Learning Tracks* record for the end of 2013–2014 (2)

	Experiential			Contextual			Generalised		
	Encountering P1i	Noticing P1ii	Responding P2i	Engaging P2ii	Participating P3i	Communicating P3ii	Remembering P4	Understanding P5, P6	Applying P7, P8
I can communicate yes		I	I						
a using behaviour		II							
b using body language		II							
c using vocalisation									
d using gesture		II							
I can communicate no		I	I						
a using behaviour		II							
b using body language		II							
c using vocalisation		II							
d using gesture		II							

Jamie's developing awareness of his environment is giving him reason to express opinions of what he wants/likes ('yes') and what he doesn't want. The class team are working with him on ways to express 'no' rather than throwing or pushing, but this is progress – see his *Learning Tracks* record where he has not always communicated 'no'.

Table 7.23   Jamie's *Learning Tracks* record for outside play

	Experiential			Contextual			Generalised		
	Encountering P1i	Noticing P1ii	Responding P2i	Engaging P2ii	Participating P3i	Communicating P3ii	Remembering P4	Understanding P5, P6	Applying P7, P8
I can go outside to play		I	II						
I can keep myself happy and active at playtime/breaktime		I	II						
a Ball play									
b Chasing games		II							
c Trike-riding		I							
d Climbing		II							
e Playground games, e.g. hopscotch									

d. New LtlO, 2015: 'I can notice and follow instructions in a known routine' (LIT 0–02a/ ENG 0–03a).

- 'I can pass an object.'
- 'I can co-operate when sharing objects during give and take activities.'

Long-term Learning Outcome: Health and Wellbeing example 1

a. Old LtLO, 2013: 'I can feed myself with limited support in a structured environment' (HWB 0–29a).

Old LtLO, 2014: 'I can respond to food which is placed in front of me and can feed myself' (HWB 0–29a).

Table 7.24   Jamie's *Learning Tracks* record for the end of 2013–2014 (3)

	Experiential			Contextual			Generalised		
	Encountering P1i	Noticing P1ii	Responding P2i	Engaging P2ii	Participating P3i	Communicating P3ii	Remembering P4	Understanding P5, P6	Applying P7, P8
I can undress myself	II	I							
a I can pull clothing off my hands		III							
b I can pull clothing off my feet		III							

		Experiential			Contextual			Generalised	
		Encountering P1i	Noticing P1ii	Responding P2i	Engaging P2ii	Participating P3i	Communicating P3ii	Remembering P4	Understanding P5, P6	Applying P7, P8
c	I can take my arms out of clothing		▋							
d	I can push trousers and pants down		▋							
e	I can remove/pull down garments with an elasticated waist									
f	I can pull clothing over my head									
g	I can unbutton a button									
I can dress myself		▋								
a	Shirt, coat, dress									
i	I can push my arms through a sleeve (DA 1 year)		▋							
ii	I can find arm holes in a T-shirt (DA 2 yrs)		▏							
iii	I can pull garments over my head (DA 2½ yrs)		▏							
iv	I can find the opening of a garment (DA 2½ yrs)									
v	I can put on a front-buttoning coat (DA 2½ yrs)									
vi	I can button one large button (DA 3yrs)									

Eating is a problematic area for Jamie. At the moment, he is refusing to have a plate placed in front of him. The class team are continuing to encourage him to tolerate food in front of him and to encourage his independence when eating it. This learning will continue, although it is not a formal target for the coming year.

His class team decided that it would be appropriate to set play activity targets for him the next year. Again, his *Learning Tracks* record supports the setting of the target.

d. Table 7.23 shows Jamie's *Learning Tracks* record for outside play.

e. New LtLO, 2015: 'I can respond to different play activities outside and increase my physical activity' (HWB 0–25a).

- 'I can take part in trike riding.'
- 'I can enjoy chasing games.'

Long-term Learning Outcome: Health and Wellbeing example 2

a. Old LtLO, 2013: 'I can complete the end stages of all dressing and undressing tasks' (HWB 0–15a).

   Old LtLO, 2014: 'I can respond to people helping me to get myself dressed' (HWB 0–15a).

b. 'I can pull garments over my head.'

   'I can push trousers down.'

c. Table 7.24 shows Jamie's *Learning Tracks* record (3).

d. New LtLO, 2015: 'I can respond when dressing and am becoming more independent when dressing' (HWB 0–15a).

   'I can find the opening of a garment.'

   'I can pull my trousers to my waist with minimal prompting.'

Jamie is making good progress in his dressing skills, helped by the motivation of going swimming and getting warm after swimming. He is taking much more notice of what is happening. He is able to finish tasks like pulling his arms through the holes in the T-shirt.

Table 7.25 Jamie's *Learning Tracks* record for the end of 2013–2014 (4)

		Experiential			Contextual			Generalised	
	Encountering P1i	Noticing P1ii	Responding P2i	Engaging P2ii	Participating P3i	Communicating P3ii	Remembering P4	Understanding P5, P6	Applying P7, P8
I can categorise/sort	▮	▮▮							
a I can sort by colour		▮▮							
b I can sort things as part of tidying up, e.g. cutlery in trays									
c I can categorise/sort for one difference/attribute with objects (balls, cars)		▮▮▮							
d I can categorise/sort for one difference/attribute (major) pictures/symbols									

Long-term Learning Outcome: Mathematics example 1

a. Old LtLO, 2013 'I can complete early sorting and matching activities' (MNU 0–20b).

Old LtLO, 2014: 'I am able to notice and am beginning to respond to simple routine directions.' (MNU 0–17a).

b. 'I can follow simple directions with symbol support.'
c. Table 7.25 shows Jamie's *Learning Tracks* record (4).
d. New LtLO, 2015: 'I can respond to collections and am beginning to sort them' (MNU 0–20b, MNU 0–20c).

'I can sort objects by colour.'

'I can sort objects with one difference' (e.g. balls and cars).

Table 7.26 Jamie's *Learning Tracks* record for the end of 2013–2014 (5)

		Experiential			Contextual			Generalised	
	Encountering P1i	Noticing P1ii	Responding P2i	Engaging P2ii	Participating P3i	Communicating P3ii	Remembering P4	Understanding P5, P6	Applying P7, P8
I can use a timetable	▮								
a I can show some anticipation of an activity in a familiar situation		▮							
b I can understand the sign 'time for'		▮							
c I understand and respond to simple routines I know		▮▮							
d I understand and can use the sign for 'finished'		▮							
e I can understand and use		▮							
i objects of reference		▮							
ii photos		▮							
iii symbols									
v text									
f I can match familiar timetable symbols									
g I know what to do next from a simple timetable strip									
h I can take a symbol down from a timetable when I have done the work		▮							
i I can manage my time using a symbol timetable		▮							
j I can follow a dressing timetable									

Long-term Learning Outcome: Mathematics example 2

a. Old LtLO, 2013: 'I can carry out a sequence of tasks from my workbox and can explore the relationship between cause and effect in my play' (MNU 0–16a).

Old LtLO, 2014: 'I can respond to my timetable' (MNU 0–10a).

b. 'I can go to my timetable without minimal support.'

'I can change what I am doing consistently.'

c. Table 7.26 shows Jamie's *Learning Tracks* record (5).
d. New LtLO, 2015: 'I can respond to my now and next timetable' (MNU 0–10a).

'I can go to my timetable without minimal support.'

'I can change what I am doing consistently.'

Jamie has shown some interest in his now and next timetable photos; he has become aware of familiar routines and these give him the information he needs to travel around the school to different activities.

The *Learning Track* exemplars and the resultant learning outcomes paint a picture of an experiential boy becoming more aware of his world and making slow but steady progress.

Case Study

Dougal: Long-term Learning Outcomes for 2014–2015

Dougal is in the Senior Unit at St Crispin's which delivers the Senior Phase of the Curriculum for Excellence, during which pupils build up a portfolio of qualifications. The philosophy of the Curriculum for Excellence is a Broad General Education up to the end of S3 (ages 3–15) where learning is described in terms of experiences and outcomes, followed by the Senior Phase where qualifications are chosen according to the abilities and interests of the pupils. Pupils' learning progresses from the experiences and outcomes to qualifications which articulate with them. Young people with SCLD need help and support in choosing their qualifications. *Learning Tracks* is a tool that teachers and parents use to make decisions about where a young person's strengths and interests lie. Since the whole document is used to make these decisions, we have not included any examples of Dougal's *Learning Tracks* in this book.

Below are listed his targets and the qualifications he is working towards. These qualifications were chosen for Dougal because he likes books, he enjoys preparing food and travelling on public transport, and he has always shown a particular ability and interest in mathematics. At this stage pupils no longer access the full curriculum, so, for example, many young people with SCLD would not be engaging in mathematical qualifications due to a lack of interest.

Long-term Learning Outcomes: Communication, Language and Literacy

Dougal will, with the appropriate level of support and resources:

- engage with, read and respond to a variety of texts, say or show which he prefers and participate in tasks associated with the texts (Scottish Qualification Authority SQA, Access 1: Listening and Responding to Simple Texts).
- Note: SQA qualifications for pupils at this level are changing from Access 1 to National 1 to match the Curriculum for Excellence.

Long-term Learning Outcomes: Health and Wellbeing

Dougal will, with the appropriate level of support and resources:

- prepare and cook a healthy hot dish for his lunch, showing basic health and safety awareness (SQA National 1, Food Preparation: Making a Healthy Hot Dish);
- try a variety of work tasks and be given opportunities to choose and practise the ones he prefers (SQA National 1, Experiencing a Work-Related Activity);

- show increased confidence and competence, making journeys to various destinations and behaving appropriately when out in the community (SQA National 1, Personal Development: Making a Personal Journey)

Long-term Learning Outcomes: Mathematics

Dougal will, with the appropriate level of support and resources:

- take a lead role in a variety of enterprise activities and will collect, sort and count the money he has helped to raise (SQA Access 1, Personal Development: Enterprise Activity);
- engage in a variety of practical everyday activities to further his functional maths skills (SQA National 1, Number Skills: Recognising Number).

These Long-term Learning Outcomes are no longer linked to the experiences and outcomes of the Curriculum for Excellence. In Scotland, this implies that one only needs to fill in *Learning Tracks* to the end of S3; after that, achievement is evidenced by qualifications. *Learning Tracks* does, however, cover experiences for children and young people to the end of schooling (16–19 years of age, depending on the country). *Learning Tracks*, once filled in for a whole school career, will give a very clear picture of the learner for transitions to the adult world.

The majority of children with SCLD will start school at 5 years of age in the experiential phase and end school at 16–19 in the contextual phase for most learning. This is because, for much school-learning to progress to the generalised phase requires an efficient declarative memory. This implies that a learner may remain at the same level of learning for several years and this is where *Learning Tracks* offers a breadth of activities.

8

Adapting *Learning Tracks*

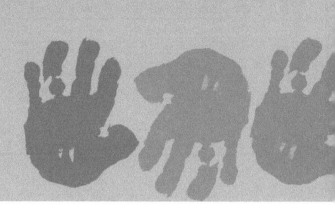

Learning Tracks was designed for our school. However, it is a simple document to adapt. Indeed, we adapt it ourselves in response to a particular child's profile and we view *Learning Tracks* as a developing document, not as a finished product. Each school/teacher that decides to use it can make it their own.

What follows below are two case studies from schools that have adapted *Learning Tracks* for their particular circumstances.

Case Study 1

An ASD provision based in a primary school south of Edinburgh

We had two children in the unit who had not reached the Early level of learning (the Curriculum for Excellence level defined as 'generally pre-school years, P1 or later for some'). We needed a tool for assessment which could identify what skills and understanding they had and aid planning for further learning. We also had some mainstream children who had particular areas of difficulties which we needed to analyse, and again identify their skills and knowledge and plan for further learning.

We reviewed *Learning Tracks* (among other assessment tools) and felt that there were features that were appropriate for our needs and features we did not need. So we changed the Experiential, Contextual and Generalised headings to the headings Experiential, Developing and Secure (Curriculum for Excellence headings which we used elsewhere in our assessment and recording) but kept the breakdown of the Experiences and outcomes (see below).

Table 8.1   Adapted example

Enjoyment and choice – within a motivating and challenging environment, developing an awareness of the relevance of texts in my life LIT 0-01a **Listening and talking** / LIT 0-11a **Reading** / LIT 0-20a **Writing** I enjoy exploring and playing with the patterns and sounds of language and can use what I learn.			
	Experiential	Developing	Secure
I can show interest in my appearance in the mirror			
I can notice changes in my face, e.g. with face painting			

(Continued)

(Continued)

	Experiential	Developing	Secure
I can change my appearance in front of the mirror			
I can watch my face closely when I change expression, open mouth, move tongue, etc. in front of the mirror			
I can show interest in other people's faces			
I can explore sound-making vocalised patterns			
I can make vocalisations			
I can watch myself when I make sounds in front of the mirror			

We started recording skills and understanding wherever the child was functioning. By keeping all the experiences and outcomes, we were able to identify learning gaps and plan for further progression.

Written by a principal teacher for ASD at the provision.

Case Study 2

An independent autism specific residential school

This school has a wide range of ability, from severe learning disabilities to no learning disability at all; all children have an ASD diagnosis. We found that the extended Bloom's taxonomy still supported recording and planning for all the children. *Learning Tracks* recording was extended upwards to include analysing, evaluating and creating. As a result of their autism, many of the more able pupils started some learning way down in encountering. It was found that these pupils frequently skipped the contextual learning and went straight from encountering to generalising; others needed to work through contextual learning. The teachers wrote the targets in the language of the extended Bloom's taxonomy.

The physical book was transferred on to a purely online system and the coding was changed to:

- E1, E2, E3, C1, C2, C3, G1, G2, G3, G4, G5 and G6.

Written by a principal teacher from the school.

Case Study 3

In-house alterations

Very few children and young people in our school use speech as their main mode of communication; however, some do. Their speech varies in clarity. Donald uses speech but he is dyspraxic and it is unclear; a VOCA or tablet/iPad would be a very useful back-up for Donald but his dyspraxia rules that out. When writing Donald's IEP, we realised that we had not included any experiences/outcomes on articulation, so we added them.

Table 8.2 Additional experiences/outcomes

	Experiential			Contextual			Generalised		
	Encountering P1i	Noticing P1ii	Responding P2i	Engaging P2ii	Participating P3i	Communicating P3ii	Remembering P4	Understanding P5, P6	Applying P7, P8
I can make meaningful vocalisations									
a I can copy sounds									
b I can join in with action songs									
c I can make myself understood to familiar listeners using speech									
d I can make myself understood to unfamiliar listeners using speech									

Adapting *Learning Tracks* for your school

The Learning Tracks booklet can be used in two ways:

- as an electronic recording and planning system where each child has a digital version of the document
- as a printed out, individual paper version – either bound or in a folder (a folder is more flexible as additional papers can be inserted in appropriate places.

We would advise a paper version because:

- it is easier to share with others, e.g. parents, therapists, learning assistants and other interested parties
- it is easier to flick through and see trends
- it is easier to add notes
- if a child transfers to another school, it is easier to pass Learning Tracks on.

Learning Tracks has two main processes for adaptation.

1. Learning Tracks has blank boxes, e.g. below. This allows new, additional or specific experiences to be added for individual schools or pupils. So before the document is finalised, an additional experience can be added – in this case a school might have jumble sales, and they might wish to add that as a social occasion. If using a paper copy, the empty box could also be written in by hand.

		Experiential			Contextual			Generalised		
Part		Encountering (P1i)	Noticing (P1ii)	Responding (P2i)	Engaging (P2ii)	Participating (P3i)	Communicating (P3ii)	Remembering (P4)	Understanding (P5, P6)	Applying (P7, P8)
1	I can celebrate my friends' birthdays									
2	I can join in social occasions									
	a dances									
	b special lunches									
	c coffee mornings									
	d parties									

Next to each box, e.g. 'a dances' is an empty box – this is for recording that the pupil has taken part in the experience with a mark of some sort, as detailed previously, but additional information can be typed or hand-written here as well. This is particularly useful for sharing important information – e.g. next to 'cinema' the fact that a pupil is scared of the dark, or in the food section, allergies or an intense dislike which can cause problems, or changes and details of progress that has been made. When such notes are added it is advised to date them.

2. A blank table is also provided (see below for excerpt) in Word format. This allows teachers to add complete new sets of Learning Experiences.

Part		Experiential			Contextual			Generalised		
		Encountering (P1i)	Noticing (P1ii)	Responding (P2i)	Engaging (P2ii)	Participating (P3i)	Communicating (P3ii)	Remembering (P4)	Understanding (P5, P6)	Applying (P7, P8)
1										
	a									
	b									
	c									
	d									
2										

These extra pages can be inserted into the appropriate section of a paper version, or saved as an appendix if an electronic copy is used.

These two processes can be used effectively by schools to customise Learning Tracks to suit their particular needs. The processes can also be used to keep Learning Tracks up to date by incorporating new learning activities as time goes on.

Conclusion

This book is a companion to the online tracking and planning booklet *Learning Tracks*.

In Part 1, the book considered what teachers and support staff need to understand in order to support the learning of children and young people with severe and complex learning disabilities.

a. Memory: learners with SCLD have impairment of the declarative memory, which results in a poor recall of verbal language and thus difficulties learning concepts based on the manipulation of language. Learners still have a reasonably unimpaired procedural memory, which allows many practical skills to be learnt, and a good visual memory, which offers an opportunity for designing supports for learning and life.
b. Child development: learners with SCLD progress through the same stages as neurotypical learners up to the point of requiring language skills. This results in a notional ceiling of some learning around three years of developmental age, as that is when many concepts and skills learnt are increasingly based on a set of developing language skills. This means that learners with SCLD function at a pre-nursery level for much of their knowledge and understanding of life.
c. Autism: many learners with SCLD are also diagnosed with an ASD and, because of their learning disabilities, even those without a diagnosis share many autistic features. It is essential to understand autistic spectrum disorder and the many strategies that can help the life of people with an ASD.

In Part 2, the book considers what the curriculum for a learner with SCLD needs to include, building on their strengths and scaffolding their weaknesses.

Learners with SCLD need to be provided with a prosthetic environment which enables them to live a fulfilling, healthy and happy life. A 'prosthetic' environment replaces 'missing parts' with artificial structures. Elements of this prosthetic environment are:

- alternative communication systems, usually using symbols replacing spoken language;
- visual timetables replacing a global understanding of life;
- strategies/rules for living, replacing social understanding and knowledge.

The curriculum needs to introduce learners with SCLD to this prosthetic environment and teach them how to use the elements proficiently. Their teachers need to scaffold that learning appropriately and *Learning Tracks* describes the different phases the learner passes through.

The curriculum needs to be full of activities which engage the learners. They will not learn anything if they do not start by encountering and engaging in a wide range of learning experiences.

The experiences have to be motivating and fun, with lots of play for learning communication. The learners should be rewarded with plenty of rest and recuperation time for their own activities between the difficult learning times.

The areas of Communication, Language and Literature, Health and Wellbeing (which includes Personal and Social Development) and Mathematics are analysed with an emphasis on using research-based teaching approaches.

In Part 3, the book describes the practicalities of using *Learning Tracks*.

The most important benefit of *Learning Tracks* is that it supplies a common framework and language for talking about children and young people's learning. The framework recognises their progress and celebrates their achievements. The document underpins the cyclical progress of assessing and planning the next steps of learning.

Learning Tracks was not designed to add another task to a teacher's list at the end of the year. It was designed to be central to the planning of learning, which always has to be based on what the learner already knows. For *Learning Tracks* to be effective in a school, it requires the staff of the school to have time to discuss the framework. Teachers need to work collaboratively to develop a shared understanding, both at the beginning of its use and over the years to retain a shared understanding and induce new staff into this understanding.

We hope that you find *Learning Tracks* helpful.

Glossary

Absences (epilepsy) An absence seizure causes a short period of 'blanking out' or staring into space. Like other kinds of seizures, they are caused by abnormal activity in a person's brain.

Adaptive Behaviour Assessment System (ABAS-II) provides a comprehensive, norm-referenced assessment of the adaptive behaviour and skills of individuals from birth to age 89. Scores for each area allow teachers and carers to evaluate areas of functioning, determine strengths and weaknesses, and specify learning objectives.

Adaptive skills are the skills an individual needs to meet the standards of personal independence and social responsibility appropriate for his/her age and cultural group.

Angelman syndrome is a chromosome disorder that causes severe learning difficulties.

Applied Behavioural Analysis (ABA) is the use of techniques and principles of positive rein-forcement (rewarding appropriate behaviour) to bring about change in behaviour.

Attachment disorder is a disorder of mood, behaviour and social relationships arising from a failure to form normal attachments to primary care-giving figures in early childhood. Children with attachment disorders have difficulty connecting to others and managing their own emotions.

Attention Deficit Hyperactivity Disorder (ADHD) is a condition characterised by inattentiveness, hyperactivity and impulsivity. Unsupported, it can lead to major social and educational exclusion.

Autistic spectrum disorder (ASD) is a complex, lifelong neurodevelopmental disability. It is characterised by difficulties in social interaction, verbal and non-verbal communication and stereo-typical or repetitive behaviours and interests. It can include sensory issues and cognitive delays.

Backward chaining Here, the adult begins the task, with the child only doing the last step. Gradually, the adult does less as the child is able to do more of the task themselves. This way, the child always gets the reward of finishing the task – for example, the adult puts the T-shirt over the child's head and helps him/her to get their arms through the holes. The child then pulls down the T-shirt at the front.

Boardmaker symbols A design program that lets the teacher make and adapt curriculum materials for students who need symbols.

Box work or workbox part of the TEACCH structured work system set up so that the learner knows exactly what s/he has to do and when it is finished.

Central Executive is the part of the working memory which controls and co-ordinates the other two parts – the verbal short-term memory and the visuospatial short-term memory.

Cerebral palsy is a condition that affects muscle control and movement. It is usually caused by an injury to the brain before, during or after birth. Children with cerebral palsy may have learning difficulties.

Child and Adolescent Mental Health Service (CAMHS) provides psychological, medical and psychosocial assessment and treatment for children and young people with mental health problems. Children at St Crispin's are usually, but not exclusively, referred to CAMHS when their behaviour becomes unmanageable.

Comforter is an object that, when played with in a repetitive stereotypical way, calms the player.

Communication books can be quite different, but in this case it is a book full of photos of common objects and activities in school and at home that a learner can point at to communicate what they want.

Comorbidity is the simultaneous existence of two or more conditions within the same person – for example, autism and Down's syndrome.

Co-ordinated Support Plan (CSP) is a statutory plan prepared by the education authority when a child or young person requires significant additional support from the education authority and from at least one other agency from outwith education in order to benefit from school education (see p. 45 for the full reference of the: Scottish Government, 2010).

Cornflour gloop is a mixture of cornflour and water which has a very satisfying gloopy consistency for sensory play.

Cri du chat syndrome is caused by a missing section of the short arm of the fifth chromosome in the body cells. Children with cri du chat may have delayed milestones, muscle weakness and heart problems.

Crisis, Aggression, Limitation and Management (CALM) is a system for the management of the use of physical restraint used in schools, hospitals adult centres, etc. Teachers and carers are trained to use it to limit the use of restraint, but if the use of restraint becomes absolutely necessary to use proscribed movements safely.

Declarative memory contains the semantic memory, which stores general knowledge about the world, language and categorical knowledge about concepts, and the episodic memory, which stores personally experienced events.

Declarative pointing is pointing to share interest in something, as opposed to imperative pointing, which is pointing because the thing is desired.

Development chart is a chart of typical milestones for a developing child. The development chart in *Learning Tracks* is based on Early Years Outcomes (see p. 79 for the full reference: DfE, 2013).

Developmental delay As an infant develops, s/he tends to meet developmental milestones as charted on a development chart. When a child fails to meet a set of the milestones within the proscribed period, they are considered to have developmental delay.

Diagnostic and Statistical Manual of Mental Disorders (DSM-IV) is the standard classification of mental disorders used by mental health professionals in the United States (see p. 59 for the full reference: American Psychiatric Association, 2000).

Disability bikes   are special needs tricycles and bicycles available to accommodate a vast array of special needs – for example, hand-pedalled recumbent tricycles make it possible for those without the use of their legs to be mobile.

Down's syndrome   is a genetic condition caused by the presence of an extra chromosome 21 in the body cells. People with Down's syndrome have some degree of learning disability.

Drop, dropping   is a behaviour where the child or young person just drops to the floor, generally in response to fearing or refusing an activity. It can often be very difficult to persuade the dropper to get up and this can be dangerous when a large young person drops in the middle of a busy road junction.

Dyspraxia   is a developmental co-ordination disorder affecting fine and/or gross motor co-ordination in children and adults. It may also affect speech.

Ear defenders   Special earphones worn by children sensitive to noise to cut out noise.

Echolalia   The repetition of words and sounds a person has heard either recently or quite a while ago. Verbal children with autism are often echolalic, which means they do use words (and sometimes even use those words appropriately), but their word choice is based on a memorised pattern.

Education, Health and Care Plan, England (EHC)   EHC plans are based on a co-ordinated assessment and planning process. The plan is designed for children and young people with special educational needs. It details a young person's health, social care and educational needs, and how they are going to be met, including the setting of short-term targets by the education provider.

Executive function   is the internal regulator of a person's behaviour through control of emotions, working memory, arousal levels and motivation.

Fight or flight or freeze   describes the behaviour when a person either runs away, hits out or shuts down in response to some event that they perceive as being dangerous.

Forest School   is a type of outdoor education in which children visit woodlands, engaging in planned activities. It is a process that offers children, young people and adults regular opportunities to achieve and develop confidence through hands-on learning in a woodland environment.

Fragile X syndrome (FXS)   is a genetic condition that causes a range of developmental problems, including learning disabilities and cognitive impairment.

Heuristic playboxes   contain interesting real-life objects for exploring – for example, sieve, egg whisk, pots and pans. Heuristic play describes the activity of babies and children as they play with and explore the properties of 'objects'. These 'objects' are things from the real world.

Individualised Educational Programme (IEP)   is a written education plan designed to meet a child's learning needs.

Information carrying word (ICW)   is any word in a sentence that *must* be understood in order to follow an instruction. An example is saying to a child 'take the teddy' with the person holding only a teddy out. The child does not have to understand a single word in this sentence because the person has shown them what they want. There are no information carrying words. However, if there was a teddy and a book and the person says 'take the teddy' the child needs to differentiate between the teddy and the book, and therefore the sentence has one information carrying word.

Intelligence Quotient   (IQ) is a score derived from one of several standardised tests designed to assess human intelligence.

Intensive interaction   is an approach to teaching the pre-speech fundamentals of communication to children and adults who have severe learning difficulties and/or autism, and who are still at an early stage of communication development.

Joint attention   is the co-ordinated attention between a child, another person and an object or event.

Object permanence   is the understanding that objects continue to exist even when they cannot be observed (seen, heard, touched, smelled or sensed in any way).

Objects of reference   used to be called object signifiers. An object of reference is an object which has a particular meaning associated with it – for example, a fork may be the object of reference for dinner. The object is closely associated with and comes to represent another object, an activity, a person or an event. These objects give the child information about what is going to happen if they are used consistently. We use them in school to represent curriculum activities or personal-care routines. The objects should have relevance for that pupil – for example, an orange armband to represent swimming is not suitable if s/he uses a completely different flotation aid.

Picture Exchange Communication System (PECS)   is a form of augmentative and alternative communication using symbols for communication.

Procedural memory   is a memory which stores skilled behaviour and actions which are usually acquired through extensive practice – for example, riding a bike.

Prosthetic environment   replaces 'missing parts' with artificial structures – for example, speech by symbols.

Proximal communication   involves adults using a range of generally non-verbal strategies to encourage children to initiate communication. Examples of the major strategies are: appropriate rough-and-tumble play; imitation of the child and the use of bursts of activity contrasted with frequent pauses giving the child the opportunity to communicate, to ask for more.

Psycho-educational profile (PEP-R)   developed by Eric Schopler offering a developmental approach to the assessment of children with autism or related developmental disorders.

Responsive teaching   is the process of stepping in and out of a learning activity to support the student's individual needs and growing independence. This process has also been referred to as scaffolding.

Rett syndrome   is a developmental disorder that affects girls almost exclusively. It is characterised by normal early growth and development followed by a slowing of development, loss of purposeful use of the hands, distinctive hand movements, slowed brain and head growth, problems with walking, seizures, and intellectual disability.

Scaffolding   is a method of teaching developed from Vygotsky's ideas that involves providing resources and support to learners as they learn new concepts. These can be withdrawn once the learners no longer need them.

Schedule   for example, work schedule – a timetable of a particular activity – for example, a music lesson or workbox session.

Sensory integration difficulties or **Sensory processing difficulties/disorder**   is character-ised by significant problems in organising sensation coming from the body, which causes difficul-ties in many areas of life.

Severe and complex learning disabilities (SCLD)/severe learning disability (SLD)   A learning disability is defined as a significant, lifelong condition present from childhood that affects an indi-vidual's development. This results in difficulties understanding information, learning new skills and coping independently. A severe learning disability is defined as having an IQ of between 20 and 34. A severe and complex learning disability is when the learning disability is comorbid with another diagnosis, such as autism.

Social stories   are story books written to accurately describe situations and activities in a way that is meaningful to the child they are written for. For example, a social story on toileting may show his/her own toilet and will use symbols and photos that the child is accustomed to using. The story guides the child through all the stages of what happens when s/he goes to the toilet in a completely personalised way.

Son-Rise   is a home-based program for children with autism spectrum disorders and other devel-opmental disabilities, which was developed by the Kaufmans for their autistic son, who is claimed to have fully recovered from his condition. The program is a parent-directed, relationship-based play therapy.

Special Educational Needs and Disability (SEND)   is where children require additional educational supports and a specialist environment to meet their needs.

Task analysis   is when tasks are analysed and broken down into small sequential steps and planned for teaching in a correct sequence, enabling the learner to learn the first step and then move on to the next step, and eventually be able to perform the complete task.

Theory of Mind   is the ability to attribute mental states – for example, beliefs, intents, desires, pretending, knowledge and so on to oneself and others, and to understand that others have beliefs, desires, intentions and perspectives that are different from one's own.

Tonic–clonic   seizures have two stages: the body initially becomes stiff and then the arms and legs begin twitching. The patient loses consciousness and some people will wet themselves. The seizure normally lasts a few minutes, but can last longer. This type of seizure is what most people think of as an epileptic fit.

Total Communication Environment   is a term invented in 1967 by Roy Holcomb in California to describe a practice in deaf education that uses a variety of approaches to communication – signing, speech, gestures, etc. – concurrently. It is considered that the main benefit to the deaf child is that it keeps open all modes of communication, enabling choice. The concept of a Total Communication Environment has been used by teachers of children with an ASD for several decades.

Treatment and Education of Autistic and Related Communication Handicapped Children (TEACCH)   was developed in the USA and is an intervention approach to help people with an ASD, and is based on understanding the learning characteristics of individuals with autism and the use of visual supports to promote meaning and independence.

Tuberous sclerosis   is a rare genetic condition that causes mainly benign (non-cancerous) tumours to develop in different parts of the body. Tumours can develop on the skin, in the brain, heart, eyes and lungs. These tumours can cause a range of other associated health conditions and complications, which include epilepsy, learning disabilities and behavioural problems such as hyperactivity or autism.

Voice Output Communication Aids (tablet, iPad) (VOCA)   These speech-generating devices (SGDs) are electronic augmentative and alternative communication systems used to supplement or replace speech for individuals with severe speech impairments, enabling them to verbally communicate their needs. SGDs are important for people who have limited means of interacting verbally as they allow individuals to become active participants in communication interactions.

Weighted waistcoat   Used for weighted therapy, which is the use of weighted products to apply weight and deep touch pressure (surface pressure) to the body thereby stimulating the proprioceptive sense enabling those who are 'sensory seeking' to relax, focus and have a greater awareness of their body.

Williams syndrome   is a developmental disorder that affects many parts of the body. It is characterised by mild to moderate learning disabilities, unique personality characteristics, distinctive facial features, and heart and cardiovascular problems.

Workbox or box work   part of the TEACCH structured work system set up so that the learner knows exactly what s/he has to do and when it is finished.

Index

Bold indicates entries within tables. Italics indicates entries within figures.